PURIFYING THE PROPHETIC

Breaking Free from the Spirit of Self-Fulfillment

R. LOREN SANDFORD

Chosen

Grand Rapids, Michigan

Published by Chosen Books
A division of Baker Publishing Group
P.O. Box 6287, Grand Rapids, MI 49516-6287
www.chosenbooks.com

Printed in the United States of America

Library of Congress Cataloging-in-Publication Data
Sandford, R. Loren.
   Purifying the prophetic : breaking free from the spirit of self-fulfillment / R. Loren Sandford.
      p.   cm.
  ISBN 10: 0-8007-9400-1 (pbk.)
  ISBN 978-0-8007-9400-2 (pbk.)
   1. Self-realization—Religious aspects—Christianity. 2. Christian life. I. Title.
BV4598.2.S25 2005
243—dc22   2005011394

No generation of believers ever stands alone. We stand on the shoulders of those who have gone before, reaching higher than they were able because they paid the price to reach higher than those on whose shoulders they stand. I therefore humbly dedicate this book to my parents, John and Paula Sandford, who cleared the way before me and taught me more about the ministry of the Lord Jesus Christ than any others ever have.

Contents

Foreword

At last! A book that is truly prophetic! A word that cries out as Elijah did, "How long will you falter between two opinions?" (1 Kings 18:21, NKJV), and calls down fire on all that is idolatrous. *Purifying the Prophetic* dramatically plucks up and breaks down, builds and plants (see Jeremiah 1:10), as Loren declares that the prophetic should.

In 1977 Paula and I wrote *The Elijah Task*, and followed that in 2002 with *Elijah Among Us*, both about the prophetic. Loren's book does it. *Purifying the Prophetic* calls down fire upon the bullock of self, saturated by the waters of our cultural worship of Baal. It comes as a fullness of repentance at a most needful time, as the Holy Spirit purges His own in preparation for the challenging days ahead.

I am not meaning to denigrate the many great prophetic books that have been published recently. Many have done a good bit of plucking up and destroying and rebuilding. But so far as I can see, none has exposed the roots of our defilement. Roots that are seen will wither and die. As none other that I have seen, this book calls down Elijah's fire to burn away our accumulated false concepts and practices. The tremendous heat here is intended by the Lord to scorch

9

us, like the sons of Levi in Malachi 3:3, "and refine them like gold and silver, so that they may present to the LORD offerings in righteousness."

Loren's chapter on the cleansing of the prophetic stream flays us alive. My hope and prayer is that we who call ourselves prophetic may be granted the humility to hear without rebellious reaction and to change without cavil. Knowing us, I fear we may find all manner of "reasonable" objections rather than come to repentance and different *modus operandi*. God wants to purify us in preparation for effectiveness in the awesome times ahead. This book may be one of the tests that define who will persevere into the new, and who will not. May I sound the warning, dear friends? Who will respond to the meaning rather than find objections and reasons to reject and discard?

Loren's chapter on worship is the finest treatise on true motivations in our approaches to God that I have ever seen. This chapter shows us the glory that can be. It calls us to worship God for His sake, to please Him rather than trying to find goose-bump experiences for ourselves! His historical review shows us painfully how our mental demands for control have suppressed the emotional fires that are the essence of true worship. I grew up in staid, orderly Congregationalism, which made of the Trinity in practice—and unfortunately in theology as well—"God, Jesus and dignity." How often I have known myself still to be bound by my training that our awesome and holy God demands propriety above all else in worship. O God, set me free!

Loren makes us see that we have been shackled by our demands for control, not free to let the Holy Spirit take us beyond our comfort zones. Often recently Paula and I have struggled with our feelings in churches that would let the Holy Spirit in if He would just behave Himself! May this book accomplish what God intends and set us free to be childlike in our expression again.

Loren has trusted God and risked our reactions in writing what can, at times, sound downright scathing. Let's see if we can prove right his trusting us as well.

In the end, it all comes down to being so touched by God's love for us that we come to want nothing else than to love and serve Him and others for His sake, free at last from self.

John Sandford

Introduction

As a prophetic book, this is not primarily a collection of predictions. Prophetic ministry is much more than that. According to the call given to Jeremiah, prophetic words uproot and plant, tear down and build up (see Jeremiah 1:10). According to Isaiah they accomplish the purposes of God, releasing His power to affect reality (see Isaiah 55:10–11). That is the spirit in which I offer this collection of words I call prophetic. I mean to offend no one, although I am certain I will offend some, and I hope to encourage many more than I offend.

The theme that binds these words together is an impassioned appeal for an entire generation of believers to renounce the culture of self-fulfillment, together with its influences on our Christian faith and practice, and to return to the profound selfless simplicity of the cross, the blood and the resurrection of Jesus. Ultimately these teach us all we need to know about what it means to be Christian. A lifetime is too short a time to plumb the depths of the bottomless love expressed there. The cross and the resurrection call us to a purity of love and faith that knows no limit. No other pursuit is worthy of our time and attention as believers. I pray that what I have written here will contribute to a needed restoration of these foundational truths in these last days.

1

Cleansing the Prophetic Stream

Interest in the prophetic has skyrocketed. Prophetic words, books, magazines and websites are multitudinous, and the number grows daily. It is not just that people are hungry for a word from God or fascinated by things spiritual. God Himself is behind this upsurge in prophetic output. With so many streams of revival flowing worldwide and so much happening so quickly on the stage of world events, it is imperative that we Christians hear from God. We must move strategically and step wisely in order to have maximum impact during this time of unprecedented opportunity. Solid prophetic input is essential.

It is appropriate, then, to begin a prophetic work by focusing on cleaning up the area of ministry of which the book claims to be a part. Too much about the prophetic has been polluted, unbalanced, misfocused and inaccurately portrayed and has produced less than stellar fruit.

Prophetic ministry has played a dominant role in my life since I was a seven-year-old child in 1958. In my childhood home, prophetic "soup" was the stuff of everyday life. We ate it for breakfast, literally, as my father brought his dreams and mystical experiences to the table many mornings for the family to consume. In those early days, we saw much good prophetic ministry, but because there were no effective mentors for my prophetic father back then, we also experienced some unbalanced insanity. Wisdom came hard. Lessons in failure could be brutal. Because of this I developed a passion for genuineness long before I came of age and have made purity in this ministry a lifelong prayer.

The heart of the current problem is our cultural self-focus and its effect on every ministry of the Church. This, in fact, will be the theme of this book: to expose this unclean cultural influence on much of the theology and practice of the Church and point to a truly biblical and godly alternative that restores a tarnished glory.

Since 1958 I have seen at least three movements, or streams, of prophetic ministry come and go—some solid, some not so solid. But no matter how unsound any branch of the stream has become, prophecy has remained a genuine anointing, even if those who give false words sometimes seem to overshadow the real thing. In the days of Micaiah (see 1 Kings 22), whom we will discuss in more detail later, four hundred prophets of the Lord gathered to deliver a false word of guidance. I do not think they consciously intended to deceive. I suspect they really thought they spoke for God. However, only one man, Micaiah, faithfully delivered the truth. In that day, four hundred voices of error could not invalidate the true ministry of the one, and so it is today. The fact that some—or perhaps even many—so-called prophetic people minister in error cannot be allowed to invalidate prophetic ministry itself. I simply believe that we can and must do better. We need this ministry.

The Prophetic Voice and Scripture

Prophetic ministry today is not—and can never be—a substitute or an addition to Scripture. The book of Acts records the inestimable value of the prophetic ministry of Agabus, who warned the early Church to prepare for famine—and the famine came. Neither then nor now could anyone have opened the pages of Scripture to read of the famine soon to come. Scripture was not designed for that. Only the living word of the prophet could bring such a warning designed for a specific time and place. Agabus spoke neither as a substitute for Scripture nor as an addition to it, but in order to accomplish what Scripture was never intended to accomplish.

Similarly the apostle Paul needed the warning Agabus gave concerning arrest and imprisonment if Paul chose to go to Jerusalem. Paul could not have opened the pages of the Scriptures available to him to read of his impending personal arrest. God did not design the written Word to provide us with that kind of living and immediate guidance to prepare us for specific life events. That kind of direction requires living revelation from a God who loves us and who is active in our lives to inform us personally, or as the Body of Christ, in specific ways. We need this ministry, but we need it to be healthy and accurate.

Impact—the Bad and the Good

Unfortunately we moderns have too seldom enjoyed the quality of prophetic ministry reported in the book of

Acts. At the turn of the millennium, for instance, we were treated to a national chorus of prophetic voices telling us the world would disintegrate on January 1, 2000, when the computers would fail—a prophecy that came to be known as the impending Y2K disaster. Well-intentioned leaders within my own church affiliation preached and counseled that churches should store up resources for the tremendous evangelistic opportunity this failure would certainly provide. Individual Christians all over the world began to stockpile food and purchase survival packages from thieves advertising on Christian radio who charged hundreds of dollars for collections of goods that would have cost less than half if purchased separately. I personally know people who moved out to places like the wilds of Montana in order to avoid the chaos they believed would come.

A few rose up to say, "It will not happen!" These stood so alone in challenging the insanity that in many cases they suffered estrangement and even ridicule from friends and colleagues. People actually left the church I pastor in Denver because I refused to engage in storing food and resources in preparation for the disaster so many prophetic voices promised would befall us.

Nothing happened on January 1, 2000, or on any day thereafter, and it had nothing to do with prayers and intercession, as some claim. The objective truth is that computers just did not work the way many said they would—and they still do not. The prophets of doom proved to be spectacularly wrong, and the Body of Christ was made to appear foolish before the world we need to be winning.

On January 1, 2000, I sat riveted to CNN all day, watching resounding nothingness roll through the time zones of the world, grieved for the damage done to the credibility of an essential ministry by the enthusiastic inaccuracies of those who claimed to speak for God. Many said, "It will not hurt to prepare, and then if nothing happens, nothing is lost." I know of at least one statement released by a consortium of leading prophetic voices that gave just that counsel. Such counsel would have been acceptable, and even wise, if it had not been prophetic voices speaking it.

Prophetic voices like these thought they spoke with caution, but many people heard nothing from that seemingly balanced approach to the possibility of a Y2K disaster except, "Be afraid. It could happen." People altered the course of their lives in response. Homes were sold and jobs abandoned. People wasted their money on emergency measures they would never need. I suspect that to this day a great many basements and storerooms remain filled with food. And all of this was in response to a "prophetic" word!

Saying "Well, it won't hurt to prepare, and then if nothing happens, nothing is lost" just does not fly when coming from the lips of a prophetic figure. People react in extreme ways because of the anointing and authority truly prophetic people carry. Those with a prophetic anointing can speak no word at all that does not dramatically affect the lives of those who hear it, irrespective of its accuracy.

People close to me in my pastoral ministry have often warned me concerning even the seemingly innocent words I speak. One compliment or insight from the lips of someone perceived to be prophetic can make a life for years to come. A negative word can similarly devastate a life.

I recall a church member who suffered from a condition that caused her vocal cords to spasm, especially when she tried to sing, which was something she loved to do and did well. I had been told by a friend of hers that the condition had progressed to a point that prevented her from singing at all. No one let me know that she had been healed. Consequently, when her name was proposed during a discussion concerning who should be drafted onto the worship team, I stated flatly, "No, I don't think so. Marsha can't sing a note." She was devastated when she heard. After a week of misery, repairing the damage required an hour of talking and praying. It mattered little that I had acted on information that had been accurate when given. What mattered was that I am perceived as carrying a prophetic mantle. My words, therefore, held a power to destroy that went way beyond the impact those same words would have had if spoken by anyone else.

On the up side, true prophetic words can set the course of lives for the good. Young Jimmy, just out of high school, was planning to buy his first car and get a low-paying job at a local Soundtrack outlet. He had thought no further and had no other dreams. It was a waste of life for such a gifted young man. God gave me grace to see into his soul, to glimpse the destiny hidden there and to peel back the layers of insecurity that held it captive.

In just twenty minutes, his life was turned. Within two weeks he had enrolled in college to pursue his bachelor's degree with the intent of heading for seminary. The fact that I could see into his life was not necessarily prophetic, as I will explain later, but the impact of the word of direction was. The prophetic word releases power to change the course of lives.

Prophets: Listen! You carry a sword! If you misuse the sword entrusted to you, the lives of the Lord's beloved children can be seriously damaged! Use it well, on the other hand, and you speak into the salvation of the world! Either way, your words carry weight to affect people in ways for which God will hold you accountable.

A Biblical Standard

In the case of Y2K, genuine, accurate, biblically grounded prophecy would have said, "Be NOT afraid. It WILL NOT happen." Agabus warned of a famine that actually came to pass. Too many of our present-day prophets warned of a disaster that did not come or cautioned concerning a disaster that might come.

What if Moses had seen the approaching Egyptian army as the people huddled in fear on the shores of the Red Sea and said, "Well, it will not hurt to prepare, so sharpen your swords and polish your shields. Then if it does not happen, we will not have lost anything"? In reality, Moses called the people to stand and witness a great deliverance and promised they would never again see the Egyptians. That was exactly what happened. Israel passed through the Red Sea and then watched in wonder as God drowned the Egyptian army. That is prophecy!

I can think of two leading figures in international prophetic ministry whose predictions I read in book form as far back as 1974. Very little of what they wrote or said has come to pass in any way, and yet the Body of Christ seems still to engage itself in everything they say, snapping up their newsletters and books with hungry anticipation and repeating everything they produce as if it came from the pages of Scripture. One wrote, for example, that the Catholic charismatic renewal would become the "charismatic revulsion" rejected by the Pope and the hierarchy. It is now thirty years later and exactly the opposite has happened.

Both of these men are genuine believers who love the Lord and lead others to Jesus. I take issue only with the nearly unchallenged inaccuracies that have flowed from them. Concerning prophetic accuracy and respect, Deuteronomy 18:21–22 says:

You may say in your heart, "How will we know the word which the LORD has not spoken?" When a prophet speaks in the name of the LORD, if the thing does not come about or come true, that is the thing which the LORD has not spoken. The prophet has spoken it presumptuously; you shall not be afraid of him.

We would do well to wise up and hold our "prophets" accountable. We should stop giving recognition and respect to those whose words consistently fail to come to pass. It would be even better if we pointed out their true gifts and encouraged them to function in them. I am not convinced that a prophet must be one hundred percent accurate to be considered genuine. My father, John Sandford, makes an excellent case with regard to this issue in his book *Elijah Among Us*. But I do believe he or she must be *substantially* accurate.

A Time like Micaiah's

Where prophetic ministry is concerned, we live in a time much like that of Micaiah, when Israel, existing as two kingdoms, faced a threat from a nation called Aram. Ahab ruled in the north of Israel, Jehoshaphat in the south. In the face of the threat from Aram, the two kings came together to discuss a military alliance.

And [Ahab] said to Jehoshaphat, "Will you go with me to battle at Ramoth-gilead?" And Jehoshaphat said to the king of Israel, "I am as you are, my people as your people, my horses as your horses." Moreover, Jehoshaphat said to the king of Israel, "Please inquire first for the word of the LORD."

1 Kings 22:4–5

Seeking divine guidance, the two kings held a prophetic convocation that drew four hundred so-called prophets of the Lord. The gathered assembly discussed the issue set before them by the kings and agreed unanimously that if the kings went up against Aram at Ramoth-gilead, a glorious victory would be achieved.

Jehoshaphat looked upon the august assembly of the prophets of the Lord and declared, in effect, "This is not God." He said in verse 7, "Is there not yet a prophet of the LORD here that we may inquire of him?" Instinctively Jehoshaphat knew that not one of those supposed prophets gathered before them spoke a genuine word, and he therefore called for a true prophet to come forward.

Ahab reluctantly admitted there was one more from whom they had not yet heard and complained in verse 8, "But I hate him, because he does not prophesy good concerning me, but evil. He is Micaiah son of Imlah."

Does this sound familiar? Who wants to hear a negative word? I want to hear good things from God about myself and my aspirations, don't you? I do not want to hear that God is opposed to my plans or that He stands against my delusions of grandeur. We want to be told only what we want to hear. We want to attend only the conference where the prophetic voice excites us, not the one that tells us the truth and truly prepares us!

At Jehoshaphat's insistence they sent for Micaiah, who said in verse 23, "The LORD has put a deceiving spirit in the mouth of all these your prophets." Notice Micaiah's language: He called them *"your* prophets," not the Lord's. He went on, "And the LORD has proclaimed disaster against you."

Definitely not what they wanted to hear! So they jailed Micaiah and went to battle anyway. There they met disaster, just as Micaiah had predicted. In fact, Ahab died.

Jehoshaphat, at least, should have known better and stood by his earlier good judgment.

If a similar situation were to present itself to the Church today, we simply would ignore the voice we did not like. That prophet would not be invited to speak at our conferences. He probably would not get off the ground with a television show. We would cut him off and relegate him to the backwaters of the ministry world because he would not excite us in the way we have come to expect and desire. He would not flatter our self-focus or our desire for great destiny.

The problem with the four hundred prophets in Micaiah's time springs from the same root as the problem in the dominant prophetic model practiced in modern Christianity. This model plays to what our hearts long to hear and draws that out of those we call prophetic.

The Same Problem Reflected Today

The problem inherent in the four hundred prophets is seen most vividly today when a crowd gathers to hear a prophet in open assembly and the prophet gives personal words from the public platform. Only once, in 1 Corinthians 14, does Scripture contain any hint of personal prophecy from a public platform. I do not believe it is categorically wrong to minister prophetically in this way; I have done it myself and find it useful on occasion. I mean only that if we practice prophetic ministry in a biblical way, then this model cannot become the dominant one. Personal prophecy in Scripture was more of a private thing, behind closed doors, except in cases where the word given addressed a leader in a way that would significantly affect more people of God. Public prophecy, on the other hand, was nearly always addressed to the nation or to groups of people rather than to individuals. While the two kings in Michaiah's time were leaders and their actions certainly affected nations, the inherent problem is the same: The prophets were playing to the kings' need for a feeling of self-importance and desire for great destiny.

I recall attending a pastors' conference in Denver in 1988 at the height of the resurgence of the prophetic movement of that time. Fifteen hundred pastors, leaders and spouses filled the auditorium, tense with anticipation and longing for the well-known prophet on the platform to individually call them out of the crowd with a word just for them. The whole atmosphere reeked of something bordering on white witchcraft born of a culturally conditioned insatiable thirst for a sense of self-importance. It certainly could not have been called a hunger for Jesus. Along with everyone else, I found myself swept along by it and received a word for my church in Idaho that never came to pass. In fact, that church no longer exists. That word was spoken by a man we called "the father of the modern prophetic movement."

In too many cases, like the prophets of Ahab, the prophet on the platform actually does nothing more than sense the hidden ambitions in the hearts of certain members of the audience and then reflect those ambitions back to them in a "prophetic word." Often it has the effect of pouring gasoline on a fire God did not start, resulting in delusions of grandeur followed by years of frustration and disappointment when, year after year, the prophetic word fails to unfold.

I have seen lives ruined by such "prophecies." One family to whom I later ministered sold their home and left solid careers and leading positions as laypeople in their community to move hundreds of miles to Denver on the strength of a "prophetic" word that they would become pastors leading a great ministry there. Not one word of it could be validated by demonstrated gifts or a track record of successful ministry, but it did flatter a need for self-importance. The prophet sensed that need, as Micaiah and the four hundred sensed the need in the hearts of the kings, and reflected it back to them in a false prophetic word. When failure inevitably came, they were devastated.

I am not denying that many of the words delivered in such settings have been accurate or that in some cases they have led to some really powerful ministry. I am just saying that, on the whole, such prophetic ministry is unbalanced in its very presentation, a dominant model suspended by the slenderest of scriptural threads.

I mentioned earlier 1 Corinthians 14, which reads, "But if a revelation is made to another who is seated . . ." (verse 30). Personal prophecy in a public setting, therefore, can be valid under certain circumstances, but an unbalanced emphasis can produce only unbalanced fruit.

Sanctified Psychic Reading

If personal prophecy from a public platform is one pillar of the dominant model in our current culture, then what I call sanctified psychic reading is the other. Again it draws support from a portion of just one verse insufficient to justify the dominant place we have given it: "The secrets of his heart are disclosed" (1 Corinthians 14:25). We use this verse to justify telling people what we "see" in them and then reveal what we have discerned of their personal history and their deepest feelings.

Such "prophecy" might sound something like, "You have been struggling for a long time with fears and uncertainties concerning your career, but God is about to make a change and lift you to a higher place." That may be true and encouraging. It might even be Spirit-inspired, but every word of it could be traced to the heart of the individual being prophesied over, in the same way that the prophetic words delivered by the four hundred prophets of Ahab reflected the desires of the kings and not the word of the Lord.

But hear me! Prophetic ministry is the word from God through men to men. It is not primarily a reading by men of what is in the hearts of men. Ability to sense and even define what is in the hearts of others does not make us prophetic. It makes us human. To learn to do it better does not make us more prophetic, but rather more fully human. We are created in the image of God as spiritual beings. Every human being, therefore, possesses the capacity—tapped or untapped—to sense the feelings and inner condition of others. Because God is Spirit, we each have a personal spirit as part of bearing His image. This is our human birthright and constitutes an essential component of our ability to exercise compassion.

Com = "with"
Passion = "feeling"
Compassion means "to feel with."

So "reading people's mail" (their hearts) does not make us prophetic. It just makes us more fully human.

In less than half an hour, almost anyone can be taught to use the burden-bearing gift resident in every believer (see Galatians 6:2) to sense the heart of another person deeply enough to give a reasonably accurate description of what might be going on inside him. Streams Ministries under John Paul Jackson, a ministry I respect very much, does this very effectively in their seminars. It is beneficial training, an awakening of the spirit, but it is not prophetic ministry. At worst it is that sanctified psychic reading flowing from the flesh of those who do it. At best it can serve the purpose of ministry in wonderfully revelatory ways, but it is not fully prophetic until it is coupled with other functions that truly reveal the plans and purposes of God and release the power to accomplish those plans and purposes. We see too little of that kind of release in prophetic ministry today.

We need to move from mere sanctified psychic reading into the genuine spirit of prophecy that, according to Jeremiah 1:10, tears down and builds up, uproots and plants. It is the word of God to accomplish His purposes.

The Problem Begins in the Pew

Much of the polluted prophetic stream begins in the pew with God's people. It takes root in those unsanctified areas of our lives to which we are so often blind and is fed by our hungry self-orientation. Like the prophets of Ahab, we hear what we want to hear, what we are prepared to hear or what our insecurities, ambitions, fears, hopes and judgments have predisposed us to hear. Just as in the days of Micaiah, our own inner desires have the power to draw inaccurate or impure words from those who may otherwise be genuinely gifted prophets. The prophet senses intuitively what is in us, then reflects it back to us in spiritual terms that we erroneously call prophecy.

I recall the time a visiting prophetic team prophesied over me at a citywide pastors' meeting. I was deep in depression and despair, in the midst of an extended season of stress and reverses in the ministry of my church. I longed for a way out. I had prayed desperately for it to end. The "prophet" picked up on all that in the spirit and reflected it back to me in eloquent terms. I was being trained, he said. My training was different than others. He said that

I had asked God, *When?* And God was saying *soon and very soon* the breakthrough and release would come.

Every bit of it was a psychic reading of what I felt and what I desired. That particular dark night of the soul lasted eight more years. So much for "soon and very soon"! In the end I hurt worse because of that "prophecy." But the inaccuracy of that word was as much my fault as it was the fault of the one who "prophesied."

Note that the first answer Micaiah gave to the kings in 1 Kings 22:15 differed not at all from the words of the four hundred false prophets. The desire of the kings to hear a positive word drew from Micaiah exactly what they wanted to hear. All he had to do was sense their deepest desires and reflect them back in the guise of a prophetic word. I suspect that the desire of the kings and the atmosphere created by the four hundred was a bit overwhelming and that, in a state of some fear, Micaiah was perhaps careless until prodded by Jehoshaphat to speak the truth, at which point he did. But only when admonished to speak what he really knew did Micaiah change his tune.

While prophetic ministry cannot be equated with sanctified psychic reading, neither does it focus on prediction, although prediction may be included. True prophetic ministry, rather, is the power to speak the word of God in such a way that things are plucked up and planted, destroyed and built up (again, see Jeremiah 1:10). True prophetic ministry releases power to set the course of lives and accomplish His Kingdom purposes.

But we have not fully understood the difference between sanctified psychic reading, which draws upon the self-oriented hopes and desires of the subject, and true prophetic words, which come from heaven to pluck up and to plant. We exalt to positions of honor and prominence those with strong burden-bearing gifts who are able to sense what is in the hearts of others but who have little sense of the Lord's true words. They simply intuit our own desires and then reflect them back to us in delusions of grandeur.

"God Told Me . . . "

As a pastor, I hear too many irresponsible claims of "God told me . . ." in the Body of Christ. It is not that God does not speak to us. He does. It is just that we have a tendency to employ the phrase cheaply to make every feeling, inclination and perception seem as though it were the voice of God. It becomes little more than sanctified emotional self-absorption! Feelings deified! I hear it all the time. "God told me to attend your church. This is my home." Three months later I hear, "God told me to leave your church and go over there." In reality God does not change His mind like that. Over the years people have tried to make me believe that God Himself told them to leave their spouses and other such immoral nonsense. The truth is that they heard the voice of their own emotions and could not or would not sort that out in the light of God's eternal Word.

A Lack of Brokenness

The problem is that too many of us have not yet paid the price to hear clearly from God. We have not yet died enough to ourselves, been broken, crushed and humbled until the flesh is taken out of the way. We still walk in the kind of insecurity that covers itself with pride, ambition and the need to be important and recognized. We remain trapped by the need for the adulation of God's people, focused on ourselves rather than on the needs of the Kingdom of God. As a result, we hear the voice of God through a filter of polluted flesh, through our own self-centered judgments, fears, hopes and dreams. Accuracy suffers. God's true voice fails to penetrate the veil of self, either in the speaker or in the ears and hearts of the listeners.

Hearing What You Want to Hear

Such a large number of us in the Body of Christ bought into all the excrement concerning the impending Y2K disaster because it made us feel important and powerful. It accessed a need in our sinful hearts and then excited and intoxicated us by means of that need. It made so many of us feel as though we had esoteric, special knowledge, the possession of which fed our sense of significance and place in the world. It played directly into the hands of the culture of self with which we have become so infected.

If you are addicted to adrenaline, you will hear what gets your blood running and your heart pounding. You will hear what stirs you up, and you will gravitate toward prophetic voices that accomplish that for you. In the process you will blind yourself to whether or not those voices have a history of accuracy. You will even forget to examine if their words passed the test of Scripture and truly advanced the overall purposes of the Kingdom of God.

If you are clinging to judgments toward authority figures in your life, you will "discern" and "hear" from God concerning flaws in leadership, whether or not those flaws really exist. Your self-focus will compel you to diminish the man or woman of God in order to exalt yourself.

A number of years ago, for instance, an erstwhile prophetess with major judgments toward men told me I was a great man in the Lord but that I had the flaw of Jimmy Swaggart, who fell into sexual sin at the height of his career. *God* had told her this, she said. In 32 years with my wife,

I have never once felt a temptation. No woman has ever had that power, and no woman ever will. In the first place, no other woman will ever have anything I want. My wife has it all. In the second place, I will not permit it. I cut it off before it can ever get through. A simple test of reality revealed the true source of her "prophetic" word. Reality checks would deliver us from all kinds of delusion if only we would subject ourselves to those checks.

Our polluted prophetic stream too often delivers what we are prepared to hear or what we want to think about ourselves. If you have problems with covenant relationship and commitment, you will hear God telling you to move from church to church. If you carry a root of insecurity and have contracted an infection of ambition or arrogance to cover it, you will hear "from God" all kinds of exalted things about yourself. You will gravitate toward prophetic voices that flatter that delusory image. You will hear these things and draw them out of people you regard as prophetic voices.

As a young pastor, I overflowed with fears and insecurities. Even more than longing to hear certain positive things from God, I was deafened by fear of the negatives He might send my way. In the late 1980s, God wanted to move me away from northern Idaho. But, obsessed with the church I had planted and the ministry I had helped my parents build at Elijah House, I did not want to entertain that idea. And so I "heard" exalted promises of growth and prosperity.

Of course, what unfolded after that was anything but growth and prosperity. God had moved on, and the glory had gone with Him. I had refused to hear what I did not want to hear and had deafened myself to what I was afraid to hear. I lacked the faith to believe that even if God told me things that did not sound good at the beginning, the outcome would be good for me in the end. A reality check—listening to good counsel—might have corrected the problem and opened my ears, sparing me the pain of struggling with a ministry God no longer blessed. I finally moved, but it took an angelic visitation in a night vision to break me loose.

Too seldom do we submit our "prophetic" perceptions to a process of genuine correction. We have too short a memory for failure in the Body of Christ and too little willingness to examine things carefully.

Unfortunately, the lesson in 1 Kings 22 is that what you *want* to hear can get you killed. Ahab died. I have seen lives destroyed, lived in pointless futility, as people have tried to live out false words given in reflection of their own unclean needs or desires. By contrast, the truth of the Lord—the valid word—brings life and freedom. This generation must shed its self-absorption to adopt a selfless focus on the Kingdom of God in order to hear what God is really saying. Only then can we move forward in power.

The Latest "Thing"

Even worse than all of this, it seems that being prophetic is the current "thing" everybody wants to be. Ability to hear from God carries with it a sense of importance in the eyes of men. We look up to those who hear from God and we want to be like them. Would it not be much healthier to aspire to gifts like service or helps, teaching or healing? It grieves me that I so seldom hear a believer express a longing to be a servant. Unhealthy spiritual ambition leads to unhealthy hearing. Pollution can seep into us by the subtlest of cracks in the structure of our character.

Illegal Activation

All true prophetic ministry must be the word of God, not the word of man. This means it flows from the heart and Spirit of the Lord and can come only from the place of intimacy with Him.

In March 2003, as the United States prepared to go to war with Iraq, I realized I had been hearing from God accurately on a number of issues. Because my fractured character in the past had not always permitted consistent accuracy, I had begun to learn to respect and rejoice in the gift.

As I drove home from a day of skiing, I suddenly knew prophetically that the ground war had begun before the news media had announced it. The Lord was calling me to prayer.

During the same period of time, I had prophesied the end of the historic drought that had gripped Colorado for seven years, and that it would begin to break in the spring of 2003. At the end of March, Colorado drank up the second largest blizzard in its history. One of my favorite ski resorts got seven feet of snow. A month later, fifty inches fell on that same resort. In May another foot of snow fell on Denver and broke limbs from nearly every tree in the metro area. The drought had apparently begun to break.

In the aftermath of all that input, and just beginning to get a bit full of myself, I began to do something illegal. It sneaked up on me so subtly I did not even see it coming. I began to *try* to sense things, to employ my natural "psychic" abilities by my own will and volition to read what was happening in the world and to sense the future. In my intimate time with the Father, He sent a strong conviction that I must never again do this, that I must never initiate perceptions by my own volition, but receive and perceive only what He would give me in intimacy with Him. Anything else would become ugly and occult.

No good thing can ever come from the exercise of my flesh, or by the activation of my own natural abilities when not called for by the Father. I am just a man. I am a prophet or a prophetic person only when called to be. The gifts of the Spirit are the gifts of the Spirit, not the gifts of human beings. We must not own them. We must not employ them on our own volition. We have not been given them for our own sake, to give us place or position, but rather to minister the pure heart of Jesus to others. The culture of self subverts and perverts that focus. Nothing of any value can flow from the flesh. Remember John 15? "Apart from Me you can do nothing" (verse 5).

Much of what is unclean in the prophetic stream comes from taking unwholesome ownership of the prophetic gift and seeking to know things in one's own spirit by means of natural abilities, rather than by the revelation of God in love relationship with Him. Accuracy begins in intimacy. In order to keep the stream clean, we must hear only what God Himself tells us in the sanctity of our intimate relationship with Him. The rest is flesh and arrogance, and I have a personal history of struggle in that regard. I have no wish to return to the woodshed of the Lord's discipline on this issue, and so I choose to receive it with gratitude when He draws me up short.

Adulation and Seduction

In our culture, truly gifted prophetic people are too often seduced by the adulation we give them. Stirring words open the door to platforms at huge conferences. Excitement fills auditoriums with eager fee-paying saints longing to hear from the prophetic man or woman of the hour. Once inundated with all that attention, the prophet often finds it exceedingly difficult to remain pure and humble. The ministry "machine" cries out for more fuel.

But what if the genuine word of God fails to sell books or fill auditoriums because the Body of Christ does not really want to hear the truth? If the prophet stumbles by means of striving to meet the expectations of his donors, his publisher, his handlers, then do we in the Body of Christ not share the responsibility for the failure?

Consequently, in our culture of self, some with genuine prophetic gifts suffer derailment by the attention and fascination we heap upon them and by the high-powered, money-thirsty ministry machines that spring up around them. I myself have a staff to pay. How can I keep the cash flowing if the words I deliver from my pulpit do not sufficiently flatter the people I serve and, therefore, incite them to give?

> Thus says the LORD concerning the prophets who lead
>   my people astray;
> When they have something to bite with their teeth,
> They cry, "Peace,"
> But against him who puts nothing in their mouths
> They declare holy war.
> Therefore it will be night for you—without vision,
> And darkness for you—without divination.
> The sun will go down on the prophets,
> And the day will become dark over them.
> The seers will be ashamed
> And the diviners will be embarrassed.
> Indeed, they will all cover their mouths
> Because there is no answer from God.
>
> Micah 3:5–7

When we allow ourselves to be seduced by this kind of pressure, the result is inaccurate prophecy and ultimately blindness and deafness to the true word of the Lord.

Maintaining brokenness and humility can be exceedingly difficult in the face of the dual pressures of finance and the adulation of the people. I have been there. I have delivered exciting words, but I also have delivered words that were not so welcome and returned home with just enough money to cover the gas it took to make the trip. I have ministered at conferences under prophetic anointing and seen people line up by the dozens to get a "word" from God by my mouth until a bodyguard made up of my friends had to rescue me by force and hustle me from the building. Heady stuff, and seductive at its heart!

After one such seductive episode, the Lord effectively fired me for letting my head get too big. I not only did not hear much for a long time, but I also spent most of that time hurting while He crucified some more flesh out of me. More than once I have been disciplined for altering the word to avoid the disapproval I knew would come if I spoke what I was really being told.

I hunger for immunity from the praises of God's people that inevitably draw me away from intimacy with Jesus and humility before Him. I want to be equally impervious to fear of their disapproval. If true brokenness and love have not become foundational and settled elements of our character, then we slip by imperceptible degrees from genuine prophetic ministry to something based in flesh. Then we really are just sensing the self-centered hopes, dreams and fascinations of the people to whom we are speaking, and we are responding to their exaltation of our position and gift. We are feeling what is in the hearts of people and speaking it out as God's word, having failed to discern the difference.

The True Prophetic Word

As I have mentioned several times, true prophetic words edify by means of plucking up and planting, destroying and building up (see Jeremiah 1:10). In 1997 at the Toronto Airport Christian Fellowship, for instance, a prophetic ministry team told my wife and me that our church would become interracial, that the races would worship together in unity and peace under our ministry and that God would show us how to pastor that kind of ministry through people He would send to teach us. We had never conceived of such a thing, so the team did not read it out of our storehouse of inner ambitions. That word released something, planted something and created something in us that we had not realized before, and we are watching it unfold today in the richly diverse nature of our congregation.

On New Year's Eve 2001, our church held a dance to ring in the New Year. At about 10:00 P.M., I noticed the Conga line that had formed on the dance floor. The faces I saw there, smiling and laughing together, were young and old, from grade school through young adult. They were rich and poor, educated and uneducated. Best of all I saw a rainbow of color—black, white, Hispanic and Native American, all laughing and playing together in love. Our worship team is racially mixed. Our staff and corps of volunteers reflect the character of our church in its mix of age, gender and race. It is wonderful and getting better all the time!

I found myself thinking back on the prophecy and wondering who had come to show us how to pastor that kind of ministry, as the prophecy had stated. No one had spoken to us specifically concerning how to do interracial ministry. Then I realized that we had come together at a heart level racially only after Jack Frost had given us a wonderful conference on the Father's love. That turned the tide, because it is the Father's love that makes us one and binds the races in peace. One Father, one Blood! After that conference, a group of African Americans joined us and taught me how to listen to and really hear their stories—something white folks seldom do. Our hearts bonded in love, which set a tone for the rest of the congregation. What the prophetic team had given us at the Toronto Airport Christian Fellowship was a true prophetic word.

The true prophetic word breaks down and builds up. It plucks up the old and plants the new. It gets us ready for the move of God and releases the power to accomplish it.

It is not that we have not seen any of that kind of prophetic word in recent days. It is just that we have seen too little of it. We have had too much of the four hundred and not enough of Micaiah, and when Micaiah has at last spoken, we have figuratively cast him into prison and refused to listen. Micaiah's word does not flatter us or cause our blood to race with adrenaline, but if we do not listen we will never come into the kind of power and presence God really desires for us, and our pursuit of the false word might get us killed.

Father, cleanse the prophetic stream. Send us servants of God so wonderfully broken and steeped in humility that they stand immune to the praises of men. Give us people who have so learned to trust You that they are able to hear whatever You have to say for the good of Your Kingdom and to know that even what sounds like bad news is good news because Your love never fails.

A Word to Pastors

We shepherds of local flocks must learn to preach prophetically. Remember that true prophecy does not simply predict things; it plucks up and plants, tears down and builds up. We must tear down the culture of self and build up the culture of the Kingdom of God. This requires courage and a form of preaching that flows from intimacy with the Father. We can no longer afford to preach what our people want to hear. We can no longer allow ourselves to preach into their "felt needs." We must preach from the mouth and heart of God what God calls us to say on the basis of His eternal written Word. It will uproot the culture of self and plant the culture of the cross. It will drive out the cult of prosperity, which is really just Baal religion recycled, and replace it with the wonder of Jesus Christ and Him crucified. It will call us home again.

A Word to the People

As a people, we are going to have to become more biblically literate, more scripturally grounded. Know the Word! Understand the Word! Study to show ourselves approved (see 2 Timothy 2:15)! We buy into so much bad prophecy because we do not know the eternal Word well enough to recognize excrement when we see it.

In 1999 one of the most well-known Christian leaders in the world came to the coliseum in Denver for a series of revival meetings, and in response to his critics he publicly cursed his enemies and their families to death. It felt like power. It went forth with spiritual force. People shouted their approval and marveled at the anointing. A small number of fellow pastors and I stood appalled that the Body of Christ and a number of our colleagues failed to recognize how out of tune with Scripture that action was. Those pastors who did not see it falsely hid behind the command not to touch the Lord's anointed.

How out of bounds! Neither that leader's public curse nor our local leadership's reluctance to correct a brother in love could stand the test of Scripture. Jesus plainly told us to bless our enemies, to bless and not to curse. Why did the Body of Christ not instantly sense the violation those words of cursing represented? Why did we not lovingly arise to correct that precious and anointed servant of God who had been so badly wounded by his critics? Sadly, no correction was offered, although a number of us called for it. The cause of revival in my city suffered a setback that day from which we did not recover for a number of years.

The written Word stands absolutely true, forming a secure hedge against delusion. No level of anointing or position can supersede that authority. When the devil tempted Jesus in the wilderness, Jesus responded with Scripture. When the devil twisted Scripture in his attempt to deceive, Jesus knew better because He knew both the Word and the Spirit of the Word.

Finally, our knowledge of the written Word of God provides the Father with a language in which to speak to us, one that is composed of biblical symbols, ideas, images, stories and parables. How can any two people understand one another without a shared framework within which to communicate? Let us learn God's language. Let us live, move and have our being within His own frame of reference. Within that God-given world of thought and feeling, our spiritual ears will hear and understand more clearly.

In Conclusion

I do not believe we can merely pray for the cleansing of the prophetic stream and expect it to happen. The culture of self and the prosperity cult that comes with it will not flee shrieking in terror simply because we want it to or because we prayed a few puny prayers. I believe we must expect, pray and even long for a cleansing judgment to come.

I speak not of punishment, but of cleansing. Biblical judgment often indicates separation of the precious from the vile. Isaiah 4:4 talks about such cleansing: "When the Lord has washed away the filth of the daughters of Zion and purged the bloodshed of Jerusalem from her midst, by the spirit of judgment and the spirit of burning . . ."

I believe every prophetic voice active in this day must choose to long for that separation of the precious from the vile, pray for it to come and then welcome it when it arrives. We must not cry, "It is the devil!" every time we encounter an apparent obstacle! Some of those obstacles have been sent by God. Some of those attacks by the devil are permitted by the Lord in order to discipline, test and correct us. None of us can afford to hold ourselves exempt from the cleansing fire.

Pray for the cleansing of the prophetic stream. The Body of Christ needs its prophetic voices to be holy, pure and functioning at full strength in order to play the role God wants them to play in this strategic time in the history of the world.

Lord, take away what is mine and give me what is Yours.

2

Refocusing Inner Healing

As God has begun to cleanse the prophetic stream, He has been moving to cleanse the hearts of His people. As early as the late 1950s, the foundational teachings for what we now know as "inner healing" began to emerge, and inner healing remains an essential component of the healing ministry today. In these last days our Father intends for His people to be clean vessels through which He can pour His love and power with intensity and effectiveness. Inner healing is a box of tools that help us move out of our brokenness and into useable holiness. Our judgments, hurts, fears and bitter roots need to be cleansed so that they do not pollute or hinder what God intends to do in winning the unsaved people of the world. Signs, wonders and prophetic ministry must be pure, rather than polluted by our own sin and hurts, so that the ministry represents the pure heart of the Savior instead of serving the ambitions and needs of those who minister them.

But as with prophetic ministry, much has gone askew in inner-healing ministry. Once again the most powerful polluting influence has been our culture of self-focus. Cultural self-absorption has torn the heart and potency out of the Western church and has subverted the direction and purpose of healing ministry. This must stop!

I am the eldest son of two of the most prominent founders of inner-healing ministry. In the 1980s, I helped in a small way to craft and refine the revelations and methods of inner healing that their ministry now teaches all over the world. We taught confession, repentance, the cross and the blood of Jesus. In the minds of a great many Christians, however, the blessing God sent as a tool for holiness, in order that the Body of Christ might minister in greater wholeness, quickly mutated into a means of simply making believers happy and self-fulfilled. Too much of the Body of Christ turned it inward and made it a sick focus on the all-important "me."

By the late 1980s, I found myself ministering to multitudes of self-absorbed saints obsessed with gazing at their own navels in search of the next great revelation that would finally deliver them from misery. Instead of hearing the call to confession and repentance for sin so that they could effectively give God's love away, Christians were blaming their parents for their brokenness and wading through the mud of endless oppression. Instead of coming to the cross to crucify sin, die and be cleansed in the blood of Jesus with resurrection power, we sought "healing" as if we were the mere victims of circumstances rather than sinners responsible for our own actions. Healing without the cross will never be anything more than a desert mirage inspiring false hope, only to disappoint at the end when it all evaporates.

Most recently, the revival stream of which I am a part has moved into an emphasis on the Father's love. Jesus came to reveal the Father, and according to John 3:16, it was His overpowering and consuming love that moved the Father to send Jesus in the first place. With this recent emphasis on the Father's love has come a renewed commitment to inner healing. I am happy for that, but it carries a danger and requires a corrective word for the sake of balance. The culture of self and the spirit behind it remain. The enemy of our soul has not given up and gone away. His favorite tactic will always be to distort and pervert the good things God gives.

In Christ

Paul

The ultimate goal of all healing of the heart and soul is that we should be "in Christ." The more I have soaked in God's Word over the years, the more I see how obsessed the apostles were with being in Christ. From apostle to apostle the wording varies, but the obsession remains and cries for definition. Paul said it in Galatians 2:20: "I have been crucified with Christ; and it is no longer I who live, but Christ lives in me; and the life which I now live in the flesh I live by faith in the Son of God, who loved me and gave Himself up for me." I find this verse to be the most foundational inner-healing passage in the Bible, but the least quoted.

Peter

What Paul said later in the letter to the Galatians (2:20), Peter exemplified when he healed the lame beggar at the gate of the temple. "I do not possess silver and gold, but what I do have I give to you: In the name of Jesus Christ the Nazarene—walk!" (Acts 3:6). No human resource could have accomplished the miracle. Peter gave him Jesus as something he very really possessed. It was unhindered union with Jesus in practical application.

Later in Peter's life he put union with Jesus in writing: "Whoever speaks, is to do so as one who is speaking the utterances of God; whoever serves is to do so as one who is serving by the strength which God supplies; so that in all things God may be glorified through Jesus Christ" (1 Peter 4:11).

If the goal of inner healing is to produce personal happiness, we will fail. If, however, the goal is the kind of union that both Peter and Paul described, we will see glorious results because it will call us beyond ourselves to give Jesus away without the blockages and brokenness that now cause us to stumble.

John

Of all the apostles, John perhaps said it best. In John 14:6, Jesus said, "I am the way, and the truth, and the life; no one comes to the Father but through Me." We have rightly cited this verse as support for some foundational doctrinal statements, but we need to see it from a different angle, one more like the heart of John and more fitting to its context. We must understand it as an issue of union with Jesus. In Him we come to the Father.

Jesus spoke not primarily of ideas or of proper confessions, although these things are certainly present in the verse. Rather, He spoke of His own Person. He Himself is the way, the truth and the life, the embodiment of all that can possibly matter to us. This is something we must

46

absorb and become, more than believe or confess. This is Jesus Himself. In union with Him we come to the Father. The ministry of inner healing must be about absorbing and becoming the nature of Jesus as we remove the blockages and strongholds that inhibit that union.

A few verses later, Jesus spoke of what would happen after His resurrection from the dead. Again the issue is union with Him. John quoted Jesus:

> "After a little while the world will no longer see Me, but you will see Me; because I live, you will live also. In that day you will know that I am in My Father, and you in Me, and I in you. . . . If anyone loves Me, he will keep My word; and My Father will love him, and We will come to him and make Our abode with him. . . . Abide in Me, and I in you. . . . He who abides in Me and I in him, he bears much fruit."
>
> John 14:19–20, 23; 15:4, 5

That last line is the key: "He who abides in Me and I in him, he bears much fruit." Oneness with Jesus opens everything in life. It stands as the key to stability, to producing things worth living for, to miracles, healings, marriages, children and everything in between.

And then there is 1 John. Much older when he wrote this, John had lived his obsession for union with Jesus for a very long time and had condensed his understanding to a razor's edge of profound simplicity. In the first chapter of 1 John, he gave a summary of everything he had learned in his lifetime of pursuing oneness with Jesus. The chapter begins with a citation of the experiential source of his knowledge; he says he is about to declare what he has seen with his eyes, heard with his ears and handled with his hands. "This is the message we have heard from Him and announce to you, that God is Light, and in Him there is no darkness at all" (1:5).

John condensed the whole Gospel to that one statement. "God is Light," but that is not the end of it. In 1 John 4:8, he said, "God is love." "God is Light" and "God is love" must therefore be understood as the same thing. What is love is light; what is not love is not light and therefore cannot be God. If we aspire to abide in Jesus and to follow after the apostolic obsession, we must abide in love.

If we would abide in love, then we must determine never to leave it, which means never leaving the presence of the One we know. Love by definition is selfless. Can our quest for inner healing be about becoming ever more selfless, removing those elements of sin and flesh that keep us self-centered? Can it be focused on removing the obstacles in our lives that prevent us from walking ever more perfectly in His selfless presence?

No Darkness in Him

As a teenager in my parents' home, I quickly learned that I was a young man morally accountable for himself under God who therefore had the freedom to experience certain kinds of sin. I could smoke if I wished (not with approval, of course), but only on condition that I must leave the house to do it. I could experiment with drugs (again, not with approval), but I could not bring them home. I had to leave the house for that, where I was also "free" to suffer the consequences if caught. I could participate in these types of sin, but to do them I had to leave the presence and protection of my parents.

In a similar way, I must leave the presence of Jesus if I am going to hate or judge or harm or hurt because in Him there can be no darkness. If I walk in that which is not love or fails to contribute to edification of others, I must leave the presence of God to do it. Wholeness enables us to remain in His presence, and this is why inner healing is important in the life of the Church.

When Peter commanded the lame beggar to rise and walk, he knew it would happen because he was truly in Christ. Because God is love, love made that miracle happen. Peter needed only to be willing to give it away. Apostolic prophecies were accurate because they were the outworking of the Father's love. While walking in that love they held no ambition, no jealousy, no fear, no need to be seen or recognized. All they wanted was Jesus. Union with Jesus had become their consuming passion, and in Him there can be no darkness.

A Balancing Word

Current streams of revival may be prophetic movements, but they must never be movements about the prophetic. They must be about revealing Jesus, which in turn is the means by which we reveal the meaning of the Father's love and demonstrate it to be real. Likewise there may be healing movements that include inner healing, but they must never become movements about healing. Healing is only an outworking, an application of the loving heart of the Father in and through His Son. We must abide in Christ and His love, soaking in that love and absorbing who He is. We must refuse to make our walk with Him an issue of self, of personal gifting, or of who gets to do what in the Church. If we will take this stand for love, we will see miracles increase in biblical proportion.

The same is true of any gift of the Spirit of God. Faith. Mercy. Tongues. Service. Giving. Words of knowledge. Words of wisdom. All these gifts are only expressions of love given not for display or to make each of us important, but for love alone. Our misunderstanding of the gifts of the Spirit and tools of healing, combined with our misuse of them as we have turned them to serve our personal needs, are chief causes of the debacles we have seen so frequently in prominent ministries over the years. Let inner healing serve to remove obstacles to the pure flow of the love we have been given. It is a means to an end, not the end itself.

Love and Faith

"If you abide in Me, and My words abide in you, ask whatever you wish, and it will be done for you" (John 15:7). Too often we have tried to make this an issue of faith: "If you believe hard enough, then your prayers will be answered." In the word-of-faith tradition, which we will examine in more depth in chapter 4, it becomes an issue of confession: "If you say the right words and confess the right things, then . . ."

But this verse is not an issue of faith, and it certainly is not an issue of confession. It is an issue of love. If I could plumb the depths of love and so thoroughly walk with Jesus that I moved always in His light, which is love, then I might learn real faith—selfless faith, not the faith that serves my personal needs and desires. That which is not love must therefore be removed. Inner healing, properly applied and received, removes that which is not love.

The realization of love produces real faith—not the other way around. If we could learn true selfless love through union with Jesus, removing all obstacles to that union through the cross and the blood accessed through confession and repentance, then we would learn true faith and we would see things happen that we could never have imagined. If we could learn to come before the Father in love for the sake of love and about love, selflessly, then we

50

would see power released to miraculously demonstrate the Father's love in the world around us. We would, in fact, find healing.

I submit that if the modern Church walks in powerlessness it is not because we hold too little faith. It is because we have not enough love. We have not enough love because we have forgotten how to be in Jesus, through whom flows the Father's love. This was the true source of the apostles' power. They were obsessed with being in Jesus, and it is not possible to be in Jesus without being in the Father's love.

It has not been a lack of faith that has restrained the demonstration of power in the Western church. It has been a lack of love. The anointing and presence of God have actually been upon us all along, but love has been lacking. The focus of our faith and of our hunger for God has been on self. Selfless love has been in short supply, and so miracles and the release of full power in biblical measure have been restrained. We have sought inner healing, for instance, for self and not for love, and so too many of us have obtained neither healing nor love.

Jesus said that those who believe would do the works He did and even greater works than He did, but all His works are the outworking of His own nature. His nature can be summed up in simple terms: "God is Light" is the same as "God is love." If we abide in the light, which is love, we can ask whatever we wish and it will be done. Love, not faith, brings the fulfillment of this promise. Inner healing must be for the attaining of the Lord's own nature that we might do His works, not for the attaining of our own happiness for the purposes of self. Inner healing must facilitate abiding in Him by cleaning up the place of abiding, so that His love can flow from us.

True love is not simply a feeling, nor is it simply a commitment. Rather, it is to absorb the nature of Jesus at the level of character. Our goal in seeking inner healing must be love, more than feeling and more than commitment, but rather as a settled element of character flowing from an experiential knowing of Jesus.

A Testimony—It Works!

In spite of a strong counseling department and a huge emphasis on inner healing, one of the most hateful and vicious churches of which I have ever been a part was my own, planted in 1992. What made it worse was that everyone involved in the hating and judging believed it was the voice of God and good discernment that had put them there.

We were drowning in navel-gazing Christians who were focused on personal healing and tearing one another apart with criticism and strife. We could not seem to generate any sort of credible outreach because our people could not get out of themselves enough to buy into it and volunteer. "When I am healed enough, then I will serve" seemed to be the constant refrain in one form or another.

After more than two decades of ministry, much of it focused on inner healing, I felt I had achieved little with my life and made little difference in the world. I cried, *Lord! What do I do?* His answer came so clearly: *Until further notice, you preach nothing but Jesus Christ and Him crucified.* I realized I had not done that. I had done as the culture had dictated. My messages had focused on how to be healed, how to have a better marriage, how to live more successfully and other culturally determined themes. It produced little sacrifice, insufficient vision and less hope.

So I answered, *Lord, I do not know how to do that.* He lovingly replied, *I will teach you.*

For the next several years, preaching was like taking joyous dictation from heaven. The cross, with all its love and personal sacrifice, leaped from every page and every line of Scripture, and I began to remember and to more deeply understand the foundation we had laid for inner healing in the cross.

I began to plumb the depths of the love embedded in Jesus' sacrifice and to see how it applies to the life of the disciple. Our congregation began to change. Over time, our Lord wonderfully transformed us from a self-centered and dying people into a congregation who could not give enough away. Missions blossomed as people eagerly volunteered for service. We began to welcome newcomers with genuine grace. Backbiting and criticizing diminished into something less than a background murmur. People attending our conferences began to rave about the sweetness and love they felt in our people. Even our counseling department took on a new energy and effectiveness as the fresh purpose infusing the church as a whole began to affect the tone of our counseling. When people seek inner healing with a purpose beyond themselves, the process moves much more quickly and becomes much more fruitful.

Congregational transformation required relentless preaching of the cross as well as an infusion of revival to penetrate the veil that self-focus had woven. Month after month, I preached on hungering for the character of Jesus and oneness with Him in His death and resurrection, explaining that the outpouring of the Spirit was first to purify us and second to send us out to share what we had been given.

Finally, we broke through the web of self that had enforced our sickness, and we came alive. Love took root in our character, and the world began to come to the warmth that at last flowed from us as a people. Love had to go beyond being merely a commitment or a doctrinal statement. It had to enter into our hearts at the level of experience through our encounter with the living Christ and our oneness with Him.

The Love of God Perfected

Jesus said in Matthew 22:37–39, "'YOU SHALL LOVE THE LORD YOUR GOD WITH ALL YOUR HEART, AND WITH ALL YOUR SOUL, AND WITH ALL YOUR MIND.' This is the great and foremost commandment. The second is like it, 'YOU SHALL LOVE YOUR NEIGHBOR AS YOURSELF.'" Loving your neighbor is inextricably bound to loving God. So it begins and ends with love given away. According to our Savior, on these two commandments depend the whole Law and the prophets (see verse 40).

John understood this: "By this we know that we have come to know Him, if we keep His commandments" (1 John 2:3). John was not concerned here with a long list of "Thou shalt not . . ." statements. It is simpler than that. He goes on in verses 4–5: "The one who says, 'I have come to know Him,' and does not keep His commandments, is a liar, and the truth is not in him; but whoever keeps His word, in him the love of God has truly been perfected."

Biblically speaking, that which is "perfect" is "perfect" when it serves the purpose for which it was designed. If the love that comes from God flows in and through us to touch others, then God's love in us has served the purpose for which it was sent and we are "perfect."

By this we know that we are in Him: the one who says he abides in Him ought himself to walk in the same manner as He walked. . . . The one who says he is in the Light and yet hates his brother is in the darkness until now.

1 John 2:5–6, 9

John thought in absolutes. No gray areas. No middle ground. He would have said that what is not love must be hate. Period. There will be no region of heaven with a sign over the gate saying "Gray area! Welcome to Paradise!"

A Remedy for Futility

John continued, "The one who loves his brother abides in the Light and there is no cause for stumbling in him" (1 John 2:10). In other words, the one who abides in the light causes no one to turn aside from Jesus. And verse 11: "But the one who hates his brother is in the darkness and walks in the darkness, and does not know where he is going because the darkness has blinded his eyes."

There is a remedy for destiny malaise, lack of direction, futility and depression. That remedy is Jesus. His nature is light. His light is love. Love is a purpose that rewrites the nature of life. He stands ready to write His nature into our nature through union with Him. Jesus stands ready to cause the Father's love to become a settled trait of character in us because we are in Him and because in Him is the fullness of the Father. In Jesus there is no darkness at all. If I am in darkness, I am not in Him. I am not in love. Inner healing, properly approached, brings us not to the absence of suffering but into the presence of a love we long to give.

We must seek the presence of Christ in oneness with Him, but with a deep and abiding purpose: to rewrite our character from the inside out until it looks and functions like His—and not for our personal happiness or fulfillment, but for the sake of ministering to others. This is the truth of and purpose for inner healing. From the beginning, His presence has been at the heart of the movement of the Spirit of God. We long to know Him, but not *just* to know Him. We want to know Him in a way that produces a result, and that result is love.

A New Commandment

In John 13, Jesus washed the disciples' feet, an outrageous act of humble servanthood. In that culture no one with any honor or self-respect would have anything to do with feet, and yet the Messiah, King of Israel, debased Himself to serve His servants in this most humiliating way. With the devastating impact of that act fresh in their hearts, Jesus told them in verse 34, "A new commandment I give to you, that you love one another, even as I have loved you, that you also love one another." "Even as" is the key phrase. It means: "In the way that I have loved you, you must love one another. In the manner that I have loved, so you must love. In the Spirit in which I have loved you, you must love."

Jesus loved as from the Father, even to the point of hideous self-sacrificial death. Connection with Jesus that carried with it the Father's radical and sacrificial love made the commandment new. Jesus said, "By this all men will know that you are My disciples, if you have love for one another" (verse 35). He spoke of the particular quality of God's love that sets it apart from being merely human love. In union with Jesus it becomes qualitatively supernatural.

A Prophetic Statement

A season of new anointing is upon us if we will rise to grasp it. It will be an anointing of love, to love as from the Father through union with Jesus at a level we have never before experienced. It will flow from an obsession with being in Christ, knowing Him and experiencing Him as being one with Him. This union with Jesus must become the focus of our quest for what we call "inner healing." As it was for the apostles, so this new anointing will consist of the substance of His life expressed through ours. This was the secret of apostolic power. Authority and power are functions and results of the Father's love flowing through Jesus and then through us by means of our union with Him. That power will increase as His love becomes a settled element of our own character held in place by Jesus because we abide in Him.

What did the apostles have that we have so obviously lacked? The answer is *love*, but not just love. It must be the love that flows from real experiential union with Jesus. We have been obsessed as a culture—even as a Christian culture—with getting and receiving that love for ourselves and have processed the gift of His love through the filter of our self-focus.

The message of the Father's love that we have so enjoyed in recent years has, therefore, been centered overwhelmingly on an incomplete vision for inner healing. The focus has been, "What did I not get as a child that has blocked my sense of the Father's love?" That is a self-focus, a receiving focus, necessary for a time in order to prepare us for what is to come, but we must grow beyond it because we are being called to a higher place. We must move from a receiving stance into a becoming and giving stance. Inner healing has a purpose beyond making us personally happy.

"God is Light and in Him is no darkness at all. . . . God is love." These two declarations express the same thing. Hate moves out when love moves in. All that is not love must be dislodged so that we can begin to truly love—not only in receiving but also in giving love with a new power and authority from the Father's heart through our union with Jesus. This must become the reason we seek inner healing—not just to be healed, but to be healed with a purpose beyond ourselves.

We who lead this renewal must shift our emphasis from teaching people how to receive and be healed to teaching them how to abide in Jesus with the goal of becoming as He is in order to love as He loves. We cannot assume that we have arrived at this goal until we see biblical levels of power and soul winning released. We are going to have to be in that love. We are going to have to plumb the depths of it. We must give no quarter to anything that is not the love that flows from and through union with Jesus. We must seek His presence with a new goal in mind: that we love not just as receivers, but as becomers and givers in full sacrificial power and authority.

To do that we are going to have to resign from the culture of self and join the culture of the cross.

3

Dethroning Baal

> For our struggle is not against flesh and blood, but against
> the rulers, against the powers, against the world forces of
> this darkness, against the spiritual forces of wickedness in
> the heavenly places.
>
> Ephesians 6:12

The real force behind the culture of self and its influence on the Church is a demonic principality. An ancient evil, it has bedeviled the people of God almost from the beginning. Its name is Baal, although it has appeared in other guises, by other names and in other places. Like its master, Satan, it specializes in deception and the creation of cultures of deception. Its favorite tactic is infiltration rather than frontal assault.

Revival History

A consistent set of themes dominated every revival from the time of Jesus until sometime in the early 1960s when the charismatic renewal began. Until the 1960s, revival always brought a renewed emphasis on the cross and the blood, both in preaching and in worship. Because of that emphasis, revival produced people of personal sacrifice. The cross modeled it and ministered the heart of our Lord as renewed believers pondered its significance. Personal sacrifice connects us experientially with the sacrificial heart of Father God. Sacrifice releases power and love. As a result, in past revivals, armies of people lined up to give in to the ways and purposes of the Lord in every way there was to give because the cross and the blood had become the way of life.

Just two examples in the last century are the Welsh Revival of 1904–1905 and the Pentecostal Revival that flowed from Azusa Street in Los Angeles beginning in 1906. Together they loosed an army of zealous missionaries upon the world. Emphasis on the cross and the blood brought about great waves of repentance, brokenhearted weeping and joyous receiving of the Lord's mercy that radically transformed lives, families, cities and entire nations.

The atmosphere of repentance and sacrifice, together with the freedom and joy that flowed from the cross and the blood, produced enormous waves of evangelism on the home front, as well as missionaries to the nations, for the simple reason that if you did not give away that which had so filled you, then you felt you might explode. Untold thousands came to Jesus as a result.

Cultural Infiltration

In the 1960s, God sent another wave of revival that intensified into the 1970s. But for the first time in history, instead of an emphasis on the cross, the blood, sacrifice and repentance, we wove the culture of self that had grown up during that revolutionary time of change into the revival. Even in the midst of an outpouring of the Spirit of God, the culture of the world seemed to inform faith more than faith informed the culture.

Instead of repenting in brokenheartedness for our sin, we came to view ourselves in a self-focused way as victims. The philosophy of the world taught us that we were not truly responsible for our ungodly and broken condition. We were victims—of circumstance, of abuse, of the actions of mothers, fathers and others—rather than sinners responsible for our own condition.

Instead of plumbing the depths of the cross to give ourselves away as living sacrifices, we created self-serving theologies like prosperity doctrine and word of faith, which have little or no root in the cross. We dressed these things up in Christian clothing, but they came from our pagan cultural values centered on self. The simplicity and selflessness of the life of the cross simply vanished.

We began to develop a more and more complicated latticework of teachings, methods and legalisms that were supposed to make us healthy, wealthy and wise. Our focus on self and self-enrichment, therefore, predictably produced no great movement of evangelism, as had every other revival God ever sent. Ultimately and for obvious reasons, our churches did not grow, except as the saints sloshed from church to church, drawn by their "felt needs" to the congregations that best met those needs.

Because self-emphasis does not and cannot work, we began to grow ever more deeply disappointed with our Christian faith and our experience of God. Now for the first time in history, depression has become one of the most common problems afflicting Christians. In 1999, I co-hosted a local television show in which the audience could call in their prayer requests to a bank of phone counselors. Relief from depression was the number one need expressed by callers.

Could it have turned out any other way? It is time to reclaim and relearn the meaning of Matthew 16:24–25:

> Then Jesus said to His disciples, "If anyone wishes to come after Me, he must deny himself, and take up his cross and follow Me. For whoever wishes to save his life will lose it; but whoever loses his life for My sake will find it."

Self-focus is killing us. We are losing our lives, but for all the wrong reasons—not for the Lord's sake, but for the pursuit of self. Self-absorption has become so much a part of our culture, and we have become so accustomed to it, that it has come to feel completely natural to us. We fail to see how deeply we have been captivated by it and have become unaware of how much we have lost.

Jezebel and Baal

One of the most destructive spirits to afflict the church is one we call "Jezebel." Churches around the world struggle with it. Jezebel was the wife of King Ahab in the Old Testament. Devoted to Baal, she opposed the true prophets of God, seeking their destruction and attempting to establish the worship of Baal in Israel. In our culture, the spirit of Jezebel manifests itself primarily as a critical, undermining, controlling, accusing spirit in the service of the idol of self that works to destroy leadership so that the Church can be neutralized. Its secondary strategy is to create suspicion and criticism between rank-and-file church members for the same reason: to neutralize and destroy. It also bears mentioning that while the biblical person Jezebel was a woman, the spirit of Jezebel is not gender-based. Those caught up in it can be of either gender.

We struggle against Jezebel, but the spirit of Jezebel is not the primary problem. Jezebel served the demon Baal, who did not cease to exist following Bible times but lives today in a new and more deceptive guise. Baal energizes the culture of self.

Israel in the Wilderness

To understand Baal in modern terms, we must study biblical history. Israel had been a people of slavery. God delivered them from oppression and led them out of Egypt to freedom, but they continued to think and feel like slaves. As slaves they saw themselves as weak victims. As victims they turned aside in fear of the giants rather than conquering and inheriting the Promised Land when God offered it to them—and then they wandered in the desert wilderness for forty years while the Lord trained the slave mentality out of them.

In order to accomplish this goal, God needed to build into them an understanding of themselves as a people. This meant learning to live for the sake of the tribe, rather than for themselves as individuals. Victims think only of themselves, but in order to survive in the desert everyone had to live for everyone else. Life had to be about serving the tribe, each individual knowing and understanding that the collective welfare of the tribe determined the welfare of the individual.

God also needed to build into them a solid dependency on—and faith in—Him. Because nothing would grow in that waterless expanse of sand, the desert could not possibly support all those thousands of people. Game for hunting and killing would have been scarce at best. The wilderness, therefore, forced them to learn to depend on God, to trust Him, to exercise a very practical faith moment by moment. Manna would be there in the morning, but because it would not last until the next day, nothing could be stored against a time of need. Day by day they had to learn to trust God for sustenance and to believe that it would be enough for them.

Supplies of water for so many people would be rapidly consumed in the dryness of the desert, leaving little choice but to trust God to provide somehow. In one case Moses brought water out of a rock. In another he miraculously purified brackish water to make it palatable.

They trusted God for daily bread while each one learned to serve his people above himself. Over time they came to understand that this way of faith and interdependence was and is the way of life. Those wilderness lessons in selflessness became the law of the Kingdom of God for time and eternity, the foundation on which the entire law of God was built in such simple terms as to love the Lord with all their heart, mind, soul and strength and their neighbors as themselves.

The Change

After forty years of desert life and faith, the time came to cross the Jordan River and conquer the land of Canaan, promised so long ago. When they crossed that border to settle the land, everything changed. Wandering nomads began to live in established homes. With the desert behind them, they could plant crops, grow livestock and depend on the harvest to provide food for them in season. Manna would not keep, but in their new land they could store up the fruit of their labor.

Crops and livestock became measures of wealth and power. No longer did they need to rely on God day to day, or so it might have seemed. Now they could trust in their fields and storehouses. Now neighbor need not live for neighbor in order to survive. Secure in the land, each individual could fend for himself. They began to lose sight of the two things most foundational to everything God wanted them to be—a people of faith and a people who understood what it meant to be given to one another in love.

Baal

The Canaanites had cultivated this land for centuries before the Israelites, successfully farming the soil and raising livestock. Over time they had developed a culture and religion of prosperity based on their farming of the land, and they had conceived a god to serve them in it whose name was Baal.

In their view, Baal ensured that the rains came, the crops grew and the cattle bore. Rituals and sacrifices made certain his favor rested on them. Then came Israel bearing a first and foremost commandment, "You shall have no other gods before Me," which really meant, "You shall have no other gods at all." Israel held a faith based on sacrifice, standing as one people, living beyond the individual for the sake of the tribe and, above all, depending solely on God for everything.

So different than the Canaanites! The Lord Himself warned them in Deuteronomy 6:10–15:

> Then it shall come about when the LORD your God brings you into the land which He swore to your fathers, Abraham, Isaac and Jacob, to give you, great and splendid cities which you did not build, and houses full of all good things which

you did not fill, and hewn cisterns which you did not dig, vineyards and olive trees which you did not plant, and you eat and are satisfied, then watch yourself, that you do not forget the LORD who brought you from the land of Egypt, out of the house of slavery. You shall fear only the LORD your God; and you shall worship Him and swear by His name. You shall not follow other gods, any of the gods of the peoples who surround you, for the LORD your God in the midst of you is a jealous God; otherwise the anger of the LORD your God will be kindled against you, and He will wipe you off the face of the earth.

In the face of what seemed to be the uncertainties of faith in a relational God, Baal seemed to offer predictability and control. Baal promised secure prosperity without the kind of exclusive devotion and self-sacrifice demanded by the one true God.

In the end, the religion of the Canaanites seduced the people of Israel and invaded the practice of their own faith. For the most part they did not believe they had abandoned God. They were simply adding something to their desert faith in order to gain an extra edge on prosperity in the land. Before it was over, they forgot where Baal ended and the Lord God began.

Baal in Modern Times

In biblical times Baal was a fertility god in an economy based on agriculture. Agricultural increase meant economic prosperity.

In modern terms that definition translates into a god of material prosperity and abundance. We no longer set up statues to Baal or perform rituals in his honor, but we do serve his agenda. It is the spirit of Baal that motivates our materialistic culture of self-fulfillment, and just as the

Israelites did, we have incorporated the worship, values and assumptions of Baal into the worship of the Church and have co-opted our core theologies to justify it.

We have done it for the same reasons Israel did. Prosperity. Self-focus. Control. Power. Instead of repentance rooted in the cross, we often practice a truncated and "cross-less" version of inner healing based on a vision of ourselves as victims not truly responsible for our sinful condition. "Poor me. It is not really my fault. I was wounded as a child." As I have said, the true ministry of inner healing takes us to the cross to die. At its heart is the repentant and contrite heart ready to be given away for the sake of others. But Baal religion erases all that.

Instead of the cross, which teaches us to lay down our lives for one another as Christ laid His life down for us, our doctrines teach us not only that the goal of our faith is to increase materially, but also that material prosperity is our Christian birthright. When we give, therefore, it is too often so that we can get—not because we have learned to love selflessly. This is Baal's way. In a true version of Christian faith, our calling is to give because giving is right, not because it "works."

In the Baalistic version of faith we have learned to practice, we no longer value a sacrificial approach to life. We live to get things, to establish ourselves in self-realization. Our marriages fail in the modern Church because we have not learned that the only way to live is to lay down our lives in sacrifice for others. Our children kill one another in our schools and fail at life because we have been so preoccupied with ourselves—in effect, serving Baal. We worked for two cars and a widescreen television while our children learned to walk and talk without us.

In my own city of Denver, Colorado, at Columbine High School, two middle-class students from economically solid homes shot up their high school and murdered their class-mates in a bloodbath that lit up the world news for weeks. I lay responsibility for that carnage squarely at the feet of our Baalistic culture of self. It is a culture gone astray in search of material prosperity at the expense of the kind of tribal oneness that would have nurtured and established our children in care for one another over the needs of self.

In too much of the Christian world, Baal has success-fully written the cross out of Christian culture and erected the idol of self-fulfillment and material prosperity in its place. Where is the blood of Jesus shed for us? Where is the life of sacrifice lived in the sharing of His death so that we might share in His life? Where are the radical saints of God who would risk everything for the Kingdom of our Lord and Christ?

We sing worship songs of victory and authority in the Lord, but is that about winning the lost and changing our world in the Father's love? Or is it about dominance over the obstacles to personal happiness that we perceive in our individual lives? How often do we really mean that we want God to help us prosper or succeed for our own sake, rather than for the Kingdom of God? It is a different thing to serve than to succeed. How often do we really consider that true victory comes only through dying to our own lives? The cross is the heart of it. There can be no resurrection life in Him until there has been a death in Him. No one can live with Him without first dying with Him.

A Remedy in the Cross and the Blood

My wife and I faced the most serious crisis of our mar-riage at about the three-year mark when we stumbled over a major dysfunction common to newlyweds. It grew from an old wound in Beth and came at a time when my own arrogant self-centeredness made me less than compassionate. The combination could have shattered us if we had allowed it. In my hardness I could easily have withdrawn from her and never reengaged. She could have become defensive and withdrawn from me.

The day we got well was the day our mutual need not to wound one another became more urgent than our personal hurt, fear or desperation. Sacrifice overcame self. On that middle ground, at the foot of the cross, we prayed, repented and forgave. God met us. In His broken body and shed blood He always meets us, but it was at the point of death to self and sacrifice for one another's sake that our healing came, not as the result of our determination to be happy, and certainly not as the product of our own will and strength. God's mercy changes things when our hearts focus no longer on self but on others, on His Kingdom and on His glorious Person.

God has written His law in the blood of the cross as the emblem of His incredible love. This law dictates that in order to live we must die to ourselves. To succeed, we must serve. To be great, we must be servants. In order to prosper, we must live to give.

Misfocused Teaching

The problem is that this life of the cross is not the flavor of Western Christianity. We are like the Israelites in Canaan, infected and compromised by a foreign influence that promises more predictability and control than the God of the Bible and demands less of us. We have seen little real repentance, while the voices crying out for it go largely unheeded. We have seen too little significant emphasis on sacrifice, giving and laying our lives down for the Lord's sake.

Instead we have fed the focus of self. Instead we have been told how to obtain our personal healings, and we have become obsessed with it. Books have been written on how to confess our way to prosperity and how to get power, without any real understanding of what that power is, much less what the power is for. Faithfulness is hard to find among believers because in our self-centeredness we come to church when we feel like it and we serve when it is convenient. With so little message of the cross, we fail to understand perseverance in times of difficulty. As a result we flee away at the first signs of real trial.

Faithfulness flows from a sense that others need what I have to give, and that their needs take precedence over my own. My ministry will be missed if I am not present. If I stay home, someone will not be touched and someone will be let down. The welfare of my tribe becomes more important to me than my own life. This is the cross! This is the fountainhead of faithfulness in love!

But this is not the driving force in our culture, or even in the Church. Our culture is about self. Then when "self" does not work—and it does not—and when the inevitable disappointment sets in, the spirit of Jezebel, the servant of Baal, floods in to feed our paranoia and need for safety. She inflames our hunger to feel important and secure until we begin to criticize, accuse and blame others for our misery. Our personal unhappiness or dissatisfaction must be someone else's fault. It could not be that we are sinners in need of grace, in need of the cross.

I am not just the pastor of our church. I am also its worship leader. For a number of years, our musicians accused me of control and arrogance, and in part they were right. The truth was that my deep-seated insecurity and fear of rejection outwardly manifested in those ways. Most arrogance and control are covers for insecurity. On their

70

part the problem grew from a need for recognition, from their own rebellion and hunger for prominence.

So the team and I set one another off, each blaming the other. Ultimately this is the work of Baal. He erases personal responsibility for sin and replaces it with a hunger for personal gain and personal satisfaction. Everyone suffers for it. For the record, God has done a work of transformation in us all, and my current team works together in peace and love.

Baal is the god of our culture, in function if not in name. We live by his twisted values. We preach his false gospel. It is a culture-wide prosperity cult, and it does not work. Baal religion must be seen as one reason the Church in America is dying in comparison to other regions of the world. We win few souls because we have abandoned the life of the cross and the blood to practice a form of faith not truly Christian at its heart.

Peter's Question

At one time even the apostle Peter was not so sure of all this. He had left behind the family fishing business to follow Jesus, sacrificing everything he knew and loved. Matthew the tax collector abandoned wealth and power to follow Jesus. In similar ways the whole group of the original twelve made huge personal sacrifices, and now Peter had begun to worry.

Matthew 19:27 quotes him: "Behold, we have left everything and followed You; what then will there be for us?" Is that not the driving question in Western culture? What is in it for me? How can I personally profit from this?

And Jesus said to them, "Truly I say to you, that you who have followed Me, in the regeneration when the Son of

Man will sit on His glorious throne, you also shall sit upon twelve thrones, judging the twelve tribes of Israel. And everyone who has left houses or brothers or sisters or father or mother or children or farms for My name's sake, will receive many times as much, and will inherit eternal life."

Matthew 19:28–29

Peter himself remembered this incident a bit differently—and more intensely—than did Matthew. The gospel of Mark is Peter's own memoirs recorded by Mark.

Peter began to say to Him, "Behold, we have left everything and followed You." Jesus said, "Truly I say to you, there is no one who has left house or brothers or sisters or mother or father or children or farms, for My sake and for the gospel's sake, but that he will receive a hundred times as much now in the present age, houses and brothers and sisters and mothers and children and farms, along with persecutions; and in the age to come, eternal life."

Mark 10:28–30

Peter had been absorbing the lesson of self-sacrifice at the feet of the Master—sacrificing all to follow Him, leaving everything behind in order to serve multitudes of people who were voraciously and demandingly hungry for the touch of God. Yet there remained in his heart the question that drives the culture of self: "If I give it all away, what will there be for me?" Jesus' answer was simple: "Everything you long for."

Our old nemesis, Baal, perpetrates upon us all the monstrous lie that we can satisfy our deepest personal desires by serving self first. In believing it, we forfeit our inheritance and make a shipwreck both of our own lives and of the purposes of God in the Church and the world.

72

Countering Baal's Lie

It is time to dethrone Baal. It is time to preach, celebrate and know Jesus Christ and Him crucified. I believe we would see a true outpouring of God's Spirit on the order of the original Pentecost if we would specifically and prayerfully renounce the service of Baal and commit ourselves to the cross of Jesus Christ in selfless sacrifice rather than the quest for self to be served. It is there in Scripture. History reveals the truth of it. It remains for us to walk in it.

It is time for another real Pentecost—an outpouring of the power of the cross and the blood that can be accessed only through broken and humbled hearts in repentance for participation in a system of thought and practice Jesus never authored. It is time for a release of the really Good News about Jesus. "For whoever wishes to save his life will lose it; but whoever loses his life for My sake will find it" (Matthew 16:25).

It is time to learn to think tribally. We are not slaves fresh out of Egypt. Neither are we Canaanites. We are children of Abraham, of the tribes of Israel, given to sacrifice before a God who loves us.

4

Reclaiming the Word of the Cross

The remedy for prophetic abuses, for the subversion of inner healing and for other imbalances yet to be outlined is simply to return to a life and faith rooted in the precious cross of our Lord. We can no longer tolerate theologies and practices that fail to flow from that foundational fountainhead.

A Self-Focused Generation

In America the current culture of self originated between the end of World War II and about 1962, when seventy million of us came into this world. They dubbed us "The Me Generation"—and justifiably so. We grew up enjoying a level of affluence no generation before us could have imagined, and so our self-focus became wedded culturally to what we came to view as our right to be prosperous, rich and affluent. We began to come of age at just about the same time the charismatic renewal gathered steam in the mainline churches and just as the culture of self began to solidify in our hearts.

Up until that time, mainline denominational churches worshipped in similar traditional ways. For most of us this form of worship was boring. Pentecostals, of course, were the exception to the rule, but we regarded them as too weird to be taken seriously. We mainliners just could not understand all the emotion, passion, enthusiasm and unrestrained expression that marked those Pentecostal meetings. Pentecostals were the uneducated, blue-collar, lower-class, not-as-good-as-we-are folks who worshipped in that run-down building on the other side of town. We were not like them!

But then the Holy Spirit began to manifest Himself in the mainline churches and everything began to change. As God came alive for us, many of us began to look and behave a lot like those Pentecostals to whom we had felt so superior such a short time before. At first it was a simple love fest with Jesus as He became for us more than just an idea or a wonderful historical figure. We entered into a living experience of the Spirit of our Savior. He healed us and gave us the gift of tongues. Worship blossomed in our hearts, and the practice of our faith changed forever.

But then the culture of self we had created began to seep into our newly revitalized faith. As a result, we began to see the whole thing as a means to get what we wanted for ourselves. We saw it as power to prosper, power to be happy, power to attain the fulfillment that had so eluded us. "Jesus loves me. He wants me to prosper."

True! But this is not the heart of the Gospel. In our self-focus we began searching for ways to make things happen for our own benefit, rather than pursuing death and sacrifice of self in union with Christ. The wonderful charismatic movement that had given us such a powerful taste of the reality of a relational God who is present for us and loves us began to be infected by the culture we had built around our self-orientation.

Two Distorted Doctrinal Mind-Sets

Many years ago my father taught me that sooner or later a person's theology will conform to his or her inner condition. How right he was! Out of our culture of self, two doctrinal mind-sets emerged that to some degree have infected nearly every branch of the faith. One is called "word of faith" and the other "prosperity doctrine." Both contain grains of truth or we would not have swallowed them. It is a good thing to say right things about God and it is a good thing to know that our Lord Jesus wants to bless us with material blessings just because He loves us. We needed those truths etched into our consciousness.

These doctrines, however, have too often built upon horrible distortions of what the Word of God actually says, until the final product has little or nothing to do with the heart of Jesus and the core of our faith. I call these aberrations not true Christianity, but Baal religion—idolatry in a contemporary form, the worship of self-focus and personal prosperity. Too often they have served the culture of self, rather than the purposes of the Kingdom of God. I am not saying that this is what the teachers of these doctrines originally meant. I am not qualified to make that call. From a pastoral perspective, I can reflect only on what these doctrines have become at the street level for the common man or woman.

Word of Faith

Word of faith basically holds that what we confess is what we get, that our words have the power to create reality. On the good side, how could we possibly fail to prosper by speaking good things about our Lord and His dealings with us? On the bad side, this doctrine has become a working of magic, a human-centered, religious-spirited, legalistic way of obtaining power over life and of making things happen for our personal benefit.

Many came to believe that the words themselves had some kind of mystical power to create, so that if we just spoke the right things with our mouths, we would either loose curses or call forth wonderful blessings by the power of the words themselves. You can watch this on *Charmed*, *Buffy the Vampire Slayer* or *Angel* every week on television. It is called witchcraft.

For the average believer, this has too often turned our faith into a mechanical thing having nothing to do with a living relationship and a dynamic love between us and a heavenly Father, a living and personal God passionately devoted to us. Worse, it cannot be reconciled with the cross of Jesus Christ.

Scriptural Distortion #1: Proverbs 18:20–21

Proverbs 18:20–21 is often quoted to support the word-of-faith doctrine: "With the fruit of a man's mouth his stomach will be satisfied; he will be satisfied with the product of his lips. Death and life are in the power of the tongue, and those who love it will eat its fruit."

In its context this passage has nothing to do with physical prosperity but addresses emotional life and relationships. The verse that precedes it speaks of a brother offended and the existence of contention in a relationship.

The context, therefore, points us beyond ourselves. Where it refers to eating the fruit of the tongue, Israel in that day believed the seat of emotion to be the bowels, from the solar plexus and downward—hence, "his stomach will be satisfied." In other words, one's emotional life will be fed to some extent by what he speaks. These verses refer not to an abundance of material things to consume but rather to what we feel emotionally, as well as to what others feel because of our words.

Emotional life and relationships are indeed affected by what we speak with our mouths. What if all I could do at home was complain about my wife or about life in general? What would that do to me, to my wife and to our relationship? Would I not "eat" the fruit of my unedifying words and feel it in the seat of my emotions? Which of us has not felt sick in the pit of his or her stomach all day over some hurtful or careless remark made to a loved one in the morning? On the other hand, what do encouragement and blessing release? I personally can live all day on one sweet compliment from my wife.

When the people of a congregation only grumble, what happens to the sense of life in that place? I once had a staff member whom no one respected because of his uncontrolled outbursts of anger. Anger expressed in words disrupted his relationships and hindered his ministry. He therefore ate the fruit of his own words and then walked in discouragement because of the attitude of the people toward him. So these verses speak neither of material prosperity nor of creating physical reality but of emotional life and relational issues.

SCRIPTURAL DISTORTION #2: ROMANS 10:8–10

"THE WORD IS NEAR YOU, IN YOUR MOUTH AND IN YOUR HEART"— that is, the word of faith which we are preaching, that if you confess with your mouth Jesus as Lord, and believe in your heart that God raised Him from the dead, you will be saved; for with the heart a person believes, resulting in righteousness, and with the mouth he confesses, resulting in salvation.

Romans 10:8–10

We have been told that we can have what we speak, what we confess with our mouths. But this verse does not say that. Clearly Romans 10:8–10 applies to our salvation, our assurance of eternity with God in heaven, and it speaks of what we come to trust at a heart level. If we believe in our hearts, trust in the Lord, cast ourselves upon the fact of the resurrected Jesus and then confess that belief aloud, eternity for us is secure. It is not about houses, cars, money, healings, curses or anything else—nor does it have anything to do with creating physical realities with our words. It is about gaining entry to an eternal reality that existed long before our mouths confessed that it did.

SCRIPTURAL DISTORTION #3: MATTHEW 12:34–37

The third Scripture used to support a word-of-faith doctrine is Matthew 12:34–37. Before reading it, please understand again that the context of any passage speaks to its meaning. Here the Pharisees had just seen Jesus cast a demon out of a man and had credited it to the devil. Jesus responded to the absurdity of their accusations in verses 31 and 32:

"Therefore I say to you, any sin and blasphemy shall be forgiven people, but blasphemy against the Spirit shall not be forgiven. Whoever speaks a word against the Son of

79

Man, it shall be forgiven him; but whoever speaks against the Holy Spirit, it shall not be forgiven him, either in this age or in the age to come."

Does the context of these verses not point to the work of the Holy Spirit and to words spoken against that work specifically?

Now verse 34: "You brood of vipers, how can you, being evil, speak what is good? For the mouth speaks out of that which fills the heart." Our words do not create reality. Rather, they reveal realities hidden in the heart. I may say that I love, for instance, but if my words are consistently negative toward a specific individual, then there can be no integrity in my claim to love. My words reveal reality.

In my own church I have often seen two people protest that they love one another, but the words that come from their mouths speak of offense and strife. The mouth speaks out of that which fills the heart. Our words reveal the truth. Specifically in these verses the words of the Pharisees revealed where they stood inwardly with reference to the power and work of the Holy Spirit.

But there is more:

"The good man brings out of his good treasure what is good; and the evil man brings out of his evil treasure what is evil. But I tell you that every careless word that people speak, they shall give an accounting for it in the day of judgment. For by your words you will be justified, and by your words you will be condemned."

verses 35–37

Jesus spoke not of just any careless word, but specifically of careless words about Himself and the Holy Spirit. The issue is not what you create by those words, but what those words reveal about the condition of your heart.

While speaking at a conference on the prophetic, I once joked, "Today I make you laugh, but tomorrow I make you miserable," because the next day's teaching addressed the crushing and breaking inherent in the training of prophetic people. The whole room laughed. Afterward I was rebuked by a pair of legalists for creating and loosing a curse by my careless words. For support they quoted this passage. So if I say the wrong things I create bad realities, and if I confess the right things I create good realities, as if the words themselves had power. Wrong! That is magic, not a living faith relationship with the living God. Words have no magical power to make things happen, but they do indicate and reveal the content of the heart.

The problem is that the culture of self seeks after control. A friend of mine tells the story of trying to communicate what I am writing in this chapter to a relative steeped in word-of-faith teaching. Rather than seeing the truth of what the Word of God really says in these passages, my friend's relative responded, "I just want a little more control than that." I rest my case.

Prosperity Doctrine

Part of prosperity doctrine is rooted in word-of-faith teaching. The other part is magic, not real faith. It is Baalism, not the teaching of the cross. It is self, not sacrifice. It focuses the motivation right where our godless culture does. When we give in order to get, the focus is not the privilege and joy of sacrifice as a gift of love to the Father but working magic to obtain personal gain. Again we sacrifice the personal, intimate relationship with a living God in order to substitute something mechanical and predictable, all in the service of the agenda of self.

THE RELATIONAL CONTEXT

"Give, and it will be given to you. They will pour into your lap a good measure—pressed down, shaken together, and running over. For by your standard of measure it will be measured to you in return" (Luke 6:38). What is the context? It is relational again—focused on the mercy and love of Father God and on selfless giving, not getting.

Accordingly the preceding verse speaks of not judging and not being judged, not condemning and not being condemned, pardoning and so being pardoned. If we give blessing and mercy, we will receive blessing and mercy in a relational context. So it is not really about personal material prosperity. It is about multiplying mercy and grace in relationships by giving selflessly. Sow mercy and grace, and mercy and grace will come back to you in greater measure.

When my wife says to me, "Honey, I forgive you," it becomes much easier for me to say, "Honey, I forgive you, too." Blessing begets blessing and love begets love. This is no mechanical magic for producing the wealth I selfishly desire for myself. It is a love-authored means of producing more love for the sake of others whose feet I am called to wash, a mercy-driven means of producing more mercy.

THE TRUE TEACHING OF JESUS

The Bible does not reveal to us a Jesus who showed much interest in providing us a formula for obtaining power or material prosperity. It reveals a Jesus who taught us to sacrifice and give mercy for the sake of sacrificing and giving mercy. The personal harvest to come as a result of these gifts of mercy and sacrifice is simply the wonderful byproduct of that kind of lifestyle of love, but it is not the purpose. Matthew 6:33 tells us that if we will serve the Kingdom of God first, then God will take care of our material needs. Put another way, we can put the Kingdom of God first because we know God will take care of our needs.

Did we miss Matthew 6:19–20?

> "Do not store up for yourselves treasures on earth, where moth and rust destroy, and where thieves break in and steal. But store up for yourselves treasures in heaven, where neither moth nor rust destroys, and where thieves do not break in or steal."

In the verses that follow these, Jesus gave us one of Scripture's most powerful exhortations to generosity, sharing and sacrifice.

Matthew also says:

> "The eye is the lamp of the body; so then if your eye is clear, your whole body will be full of light. But if your eye is bad, your whole body will be full of darkness. If then the light that is in you is darkness, how great is the darkness!"
>
> Matthew 6:22–23

This is no reference to some mysterious metaphysical quality resident in the human eye. In Bible times, a generous man would be spoken of as having a good or clear eye, while it would be said of a stingy man that he had a bad eye. It is about giving, or not giving, and the light or darkness that results in our inner life. Life selfishly lived leads to darkness and depression.

Matthew 10:38–39:

> "And he who does not take his cross and follow after Me is not worthy of Me. He who has found his life will lose it, and he who has lost his life for My sake will find it."

Translation: You will never find yourself by being self-focused. Sacrifice of self is the way of life.

> "If anyone wishes to come after Me, he must deny himself, and take up his cross and follow Me. For whoever wishes to save his life will lose it; but whoever loses his life for My sake will find it. For what will it profit a man if he gains the whole world and forfeits his soul? Or what will a man give in exchange for his soul?"
>
> Matthew 16:24–26

> "Whoever then humbles himself as this child, he is the greatest in the kingdom of heaven. And whoever receives one such child in My name receives Me."
>
> Matthew 18:4–5

It is time to bring down Baal religion, the self-serving fertility and prosperity cult. It is nothing more than dead religion steeped in human effort, which never could and never will save us. Our faith has its center in the cross, the emblem of ultimate sacrifice in love for others. Jesus came to teach us how to live well by dying, by sacrificing. "Blessed are the poor in spirit, for theirs is the kingdom of heaven" (Matthew 5:3). Putting the cross back at the center of our faith means forgiveness, mercy, sacrifice and death of self. The focus must become not how we can realize ourselves, but how we can sacrifice ourselves.

In Matthew 19:21, Jesus said to the rich young ruler, "If you wish to be complete, go and sell your possessions and give to the poor, and you will have treasure in heaven; and come, follow Me." This young man's prosperity gospel prevented him from following Jesus. We must put the cross, and not the idol of self and prosperity, back at the forefront.

According to Paul

The apostle Paul said:

For the word of the cross is foolishness to those who are perishing, but to us who are being saved it is the power of God.

1 Corinthians 1:18

For I determined to know nothing among you except Jesus Christ, and Him crucified. I was with you in weakness and in fear and in much trembling, and my message and my preaching were not in persuasive words of wisdom, but in demonstration of the Spirit and of power, so that your faith would not rest on the wisdom of men, but on the power of God.

1 Corinthians 2:2–5

The power is where? In the words men and women speak? No. It is in the cross and in the very Person of Jesus. Our faith rests not in the power of what we say with our mouths, but in what Jesus did and in what Jesus does.

I have been crucified with Christ; and it is no longer I who live, but Christ lives in me; and the life which I now live in the flesh I live by faith in the Son of God, who loved me and gave Himself up for me.

Galatians 2:20

But whatever things were gain to me, those things I have counted as loss for the sake of Christ. More than that, I count all things to be loss in view of the surpassing value of knowing Christ Jesus my Lord, for whom I have suffered the loss of all things, and count them but rubbish so that I may gain Christ.

Philippians 3:7–8

Some of us need to ask ourselves, "Am I really a Christian? Am I really in the faith? Or am I just a camp follower?" Is it Christian faith we have practiced or just sanctified Baalism? Or are we syncretists, blending the culture of the world with the Gospel and calling it Christian?

Jesus Lifted Up

I long for the Church to be a place where Jesus is lifted up, but I long for Him to be lifted up as in Scripture, on that cross and in His resurrection. We must learn from the cross, drink from it and participate in the resurrection that comes after it, because of it and from it. Church must not be a place where we learn only how to prosper self, but where we discover how to transcend self and become as Jesus is. "I have died," declared the apostle, but that is not the end of the story. There follows a life in Him better than any life any of us has experienced.

Baal told us a lie. In the days to come, our Lord wants His Church cleansed of the culture of self and the Baalistic misinterpretations of His Word that have come with it. He will give His blessing to those who determine to revel in His sacrifice—to live, preach and understand Jesus Christ and Him crucified.

If we will commit to this truly Jesus-centered emphasis, we will change the world. "And I, if I am lifted up from the earth, will draw all men to Myself" (John 12:32). "Lifted up" means more than using His name in every other sentence. It is the idiom Jesus employed to refer to His own death as He was lifted up on the cross. If we will live as He lived, embodying in ourselves and the conduct of our lives His true self-sacrificial nature as epitomized in the cross, then all men will be drawn to Him.

Finally, witness the early disciples who sold whatever they possessed, sacrificing selflessly in support of those who had need, putting real feet to the love they experienced in His Spirit (see Acts 2). In verse 47 they were "praising God and having favor with all the people. And the Lord was adding to their number day by day those who were being saved." If Jesus is lifted up by any means reflective of His cross, He will draw all to Himself. We must put the cross and not the idol of prosperity back at the center of our faith.

5

Loving the Blood of Jesus

———————•———————

Along with the cross as a focus of life and as a remedy for self-focus stands the necessity for a renewed emphasis on the blood of Jesus. Like the cross, it calls us to selfless sacrifice and away from the prison of our misfocused culture.

We live in a time awash in Christian teaching. Never before have so many books been available from such a variety of outlets ranging from the shopping mall to the Internet. Never before has it been possible to switch on the television or the radio any time, day or night, and find Christian programming at several locations on the dial. We should be well educated and grounded in God's Word.

But we are not. In fact, most Christians remain biblically illiterate. Apalling numbers of ostensible Bible-believing Christians espouse a hodgepodge of unbiblical docrines ranging from the belief that Satan is "not a living being but is a symbol of evil" to the idea that if a person is good enough, he or she can earn a place in heaven. A significant percentage reject moral absolutes, and even fewer say they base their personal life decisions on the principles of Scripture. These are just a few of the frightening trends that show us the erosion of something precious and foundational from our faith in Christ and from His Word.

Church growth figures are even more frightening. As a percentage of the population, church attendees have been in serious decline for a number of years. Every year in America, three thousand churches are planted, while four thousand close. Even in the face of all that teaching, how have we come to this sad place?

You know the answer. You have been reading it in these pages, so you understand. It is another variation on our culture of self that renders us functionally deaf to the heart of the Gospel.

No Foundation in the Cross and the Blood

Envision a 21-year-old giving his life to Jesus and spending the next ten years listening to preaching and teaching in church, on the radio, in books and on television. What does he hear? Based on what he sees and hears, what is he led to understand about the Christian faith?

He probably thinks his faith is about victory, power, obtaining wealth and focusing on personal well-being by working certain principles. He may hear a lot of talk about the authority of the believer. He will hear these things because the real religion of America and the West is the cult of self and prosperity. Instead of plumbing the depths of the scandal of the cross—which Paul said in 1 Corinthians 1:23 is "Christ crucified, to Jews a stumbling block and to Gentiles foolishness"—the Church has spent the last few decades catering to this worldly cult and serving the demands of those caught up in it. Note the continuation of the thought in verses 24 and 25: ". . . but to those who are the called, both Jews and Greeks, Christ the power of God and the wisdom of God. Because the foolishness of God is wiser than men, and the weakness of God is stronger than men."

Unfortunately, our young man is lost to this. For the most part he has not heard this message, except in occasional whispers or in brief and polite nods in the direction of our historic faith. As he continues to watch Christian television and listen to Christian radio, he may even come to understand that an essential element of his faith is hating homosexuals, abortionists, liberal politicians and the entertainment industry. We picket, protest, condemn and pull away from these people. Somewhere in the back of his mind, he may instinctively understand that something is wrong with this picture and may begin to question his identity as a Christian.

What he probably does not hear is a clear and passionate message of the cross and the blood of Jesus, together with their implications for the life of the believer. He knows that Jesus died for his sin, but he does not really comprehend what that means. The concept holds no real content for him because it is seldom explained in any depth that would change his life or confront the infiltration of the culture into his worldview.

The trouble is that all the formulas that have formed the bulk of the message he has heard sooner or later just do not work. He thought it was all about power, prosperity, ease of living and the authority of the believer, but the time must come when God sends him an experience like Job's. Inevitably he must face losses of some kind, perhaps over an extended period of time. Because the Church has given him no grid for processing hurt and hardship, because we have no workable theology for suffering, disillusionment sets in and he begins to believe his Christian faith has failed him.

He does not know that it failed him because it had no foundation in the cross and the blood. It was built on methods and magical principles designed to serve personal needs, rather than on the loss of life that results in finding it. When those methods and principles fail, he begins to question his God because contemporary Christian teaching gave him no adequate theological framework with which to process adversity.

As he questions these things, he finds that Christians are not the only ones communicating these same health, wealth and prosperity messages, although others couch them in different terms. He begins to think that maybe there are other ways to get to God that might be just as good as Christianity. In the process he loses his sense of the distinctives of Christian faith because nobody ever really taught them to him.

At the point that he surrenders his sense of the uniqueness of what God has done in Jesus, at the point that he believes anyone can come to God by any means other than the cross of Christ, he has invalidated everything Jesus came to do and be and has begun to follow a different "christ," if he still thinks of following Christ at all. Baal wins. Why? Because in too many places and in too many ways we have neither practiced nor taught essential Christianity in the Western world.

Loving the Blood

I earnestly sought the Lord for an answer concerning how we had come to this sad place. He answered clearly,

It is because they longed more for My power than for My blood. How true, and how rooted in self!

Consider the church in Corinth two thousand years ago. Like us, the Corinthian church was hungry for power, corrupted by prosperity and loved great orators and clever words! The apostle Paul wrote to correct them: "I did not come with superiority of speech or of wisdom, proclaiming to you the testimony of God. For I determined to know nothing among you except Jesus Christ, and Him crucified" (1 Corinthians 2:1–2).

This speaks of Jesus' blood that was shed when they whipped Him with weighted thongs that tore the flesh from his back in strips until the bones were exposed. It speaks of the blood that flowed from His hands, feet and side as He hung on the cross. This blood brings life and healing. This blood cleanses us from our sin.

Paul said to the Romans, "Having now been justified by His blood, we shall be saved from the wrath of God through Him" (Romans 5:9). The new covenant, the new and unprecedented relationship with God that Jesus brought, is a new covenant in His blood. At the Last Supper, He gave them the cup of wine and said, "This cup which is poured out for you is the new covenant in My blood" (Luke 22:20).

Until we understand the price He paid in blood and the power of that blood to break the back of sin and cleanse us from it, we will never really love Jesus, much less come to know and follow after Him in a wonderfully sacrificial life like His. We can neither love nor know Him without understanding what He suffered, for whom He did it and why.

A Personal Testimony

Brought up in church as a preacher's kid, I knew all the facts of the faith. I considered myself a Christian but struggled with the idea of actually feeling an emotional love for Jesus. It just was not there. Finally one day in 1971, my future bride and I were watching television in her college dormitory room. It was a pseudo-documentary news piece on the crucifixion of Jesus in which the reporter went "back in time" to interview and report on the events as they happened. I will never forget the sound of the lash and the cries of pain coming from the building behind the reporter as he coolly and objectively described the scourging.

Suddenly it all became real for me—what it cost Him, why He did it and for whom—and I began to weep with love and revelation. I buried my head in Beth's lap and let it all come out. I have been in love with my Savior ever since. I believe that was the day I was actually born again, when I gave myself over to serve Him and everything changed. Life acquired a different meaning after that. This is the definition of being born again, isn't it? Not just words, but inner change leading to outward evidence of that change! Jesus Christ and Him crucified! There can be no other Gospel!

Isaiah 53

"Surely our griefs He Himself bore, and our sorrows He carried. . . . But He was pierced through for our transgressions" (Isaiah 53:4–5). At the end, as He hung dying on the cross, they ran a sword through His ribs into His heart to make certain He had died. "He was crushed for our iniquities; the chastening for our well-being fell upon Him, and by His scourging we are healed" (verse 5 continued).

We keep crying, "Let the power of God heal us! Let the power of God raise the dead! Let the power of God restore blind eyes! Let the power of God change my life!" But the prophecy was not that we would be healed by His power.

The prophecy was that we would be healed by His scourging. As His blood was shed, our griefs and sorrows would be carried away. As He suffered in our place, paying the price for our sin, we would be restored.

Hidden in the blood is the selfless sacrifice we all need to take into ourselves as the precious character of Jesus. Think of the blood of Jesus as an effective antidote to the infiltration of the self-centered cultural disease I call Baalism.

The promised healing is threefold—physical, emotional and spiritual. In Mark 2, four men brought a quadriplegic to Jesus, bearing him on a stretcher. In verse 5, Jesus said a strange thing: "Son, your sins are forgiven." That set off an offense among the Pharisees who thought Jesus presumptuous. In verses 10–11, Jesus again connected forgiveness of sin with the healing of the paralytic: "'But so that you may know that the Son of Man has authority on earth to forgive sins'—He said to the paralytic, 'I say to you, get up, pick up your pallet and go home.'"

The healing of the paralytic stood as proof that Jesus had authority to forgive. Power for healing remains intimately connected with authority to forgive. Ultimate, full and final forgiveness was won the day they scourged and crucified our Lord, the day He shed His sacrificial blood. "Therefore, confess your sins to one another, and pray for one another so that you may be healed" (James 5:16). Healing and forgiveness intertwine because of the threefold nature of the gift in its physical, emotional and spiritual dimensions. Forgiveness flows from the blood of Jesus, from the cross. Our first calling as believers must therefore be to minister what He has already won.

I am not saying that all people who fall sick or need healing got that way because of personal sin. I am saying that healing flows primarily from the blood shed selflessly for forgiveness. Suffering entered the world because the self-centered sin of mankind brought it in. The blood of Jesus cleanses it, but under the influence of the demon Baal, we have hungered for power and success at the expense of the self-sacrificial message of the blood.

"By His scourging we are healed. All of us like sheep have gone astray" (Isaiah 53:5–6). Is any one of us good enough? Hardly. If that were possible, Jesus would never have come and there would have been no need for the cross. Each of us has turned to His own way, seduced by the culture of self, "but the LORD has caused the iniquity of us all to fall on Him" (verse 6). In the blood of Jesus, we overcome self.

The Blood Is Everything

The following passage is first about the celebration of Communion, the Lord's Supper. Figuratively I believe it also speaks of taking into our own character all that the blood of Jesus represents in forgiveness, sacrifice and love.

> "Truly, truly, I say to you, unless you eat the flesh of the Son of Man and drink His blood, you have no life in yourselves. He who eats My flesh and drinks My blood has eternal life, and I will raise him up on the last day. For My flesh is true food, and My blood is true drink. He who eats My flesh and drinks My blood abides in Me, and I in him."
>
> John 6:53–56

The blood of Jesus is everything to the Christian. Without His character imparted through His death in and through His blood, we can never truly live.

"In Him we have redemption through His blood, the forgiveness of our trespasses, according to the riches of His grace. . . . But now in Christ Jesus you who formerly were far off have been brought near by the blood of Christ" (Ephesians 1:7; 2:13). The unholy cannot enter the raw presence of the holy. Only by the shed blood of Jesus have we been cleansed of unholiness and brought near to God.

No one comes to the Father except by Jesus. Only in Jesus has perfected sacrificial blood been shed once for all to cleanse us from unholiness. Healing follows after forgiveness and holiness. Why? Because sickness in all its forms is a manifestation of the sinful state of mankind that has now been covered by His blood. Wholeness is a manifestation of what we have been redeemed into by the shed blood.

A New Emphasis

Let's put a new emphasis on the cross and the blood of Jesus, but not in order to obtain power, health, wealth and prosperity. Certainly let's not do it to further our search for self! Let's do it in order to understand the depth of the meaning of the cross. We must take these things into ourselves until the content of His sacrifice takes possession of our character, until we become within ourselves what the blood means in sacrifice, love, dying and rising. Let's shift our focus there and meditate on it because in pondering the blood and its meaning, we become more like Him. *Father, teach us to love the blood more than the power.*

I want to see if, in seeking the blood over the power, we receive a new outpouring of healings and miracles in the Church. I believe Scripture shows us that one follows the other. If forgiveness of sin formed an essential part of the healing of the paralytic, would it not make sense that a holy and forgiven people, pondering the blood and letting it cleanse them from sin, would see healing released in their midst? Cleansing from sin implies change of character, and character matters.

Previous generations of believers understood what I am saying. Past revivals were all about the blood of Jesus. Salvations, miracles and tremendous missions movements followed as people gave themselves away. They wrote wonderful, incredible songs about it, and it changed their world.

> O the blood of Jesus,
> O the blood of Jesus,
> O the blood of Jesus
> That washes white as snow.

6

The Rising Tide of Hatred

The self-focused culture of the West is invading the rest of the world. The inevitable result is an unprecedented increase of hatred across a broad range of nations. Self-focus brings loss of love, which leads to hatred, so hatred is the ultimate form of self-focus. When men and women become lovers of self, they become unloving and hateful.

> But realize this, that in the last days difficult times will come. For men will be lovers of self, lovers of money, boastful, arrogant, revilers, disobedient to parents, ungrateful, unholy, unloving, irreconcilable, malicious gossips, without self-control, brutal, haters of good, treacherous, reckless, conceited, lovers of pleasure rather than lovers of God, holding to a form of godliness, although they have denied its power; Avoid such men as these.
>
> 2 Timothy 3:1–5

The last item on Paul's list is powerless religion, which explains why so many more miracles seem to manifest in third-world missions settings where Western culture has not yet fully penetrated. Demonic inspiration can produce only demonic fruit. Unhealthy self-focus can only destroy.

Paul Described the Church Today

Paul prophesied our decay in his letter to Timothy, and in spite of revivals in many parts of the world, the Church in the West seems to be leading the way into the great falling away: "At that time many will fall away and will betray one another and hate one another" (Matthew 24:10).

I grieve that Paul's description of the Church in the last days fits my own experience with the Church at large for most of my life, and I see it growing progressively worse. Masses of people are caught in the trap of the culture of self, energized by Baal, the prosperity god. They attend church as believers but exhibit little of the character of Jesus on a daily basis. Unfortunately, too many of the churches they attend cater to the culture of self at the expense of the preaching of the cross.

Overall, the Church in America has been in measurable decline for many years, even as our media influence and publishing efforts have burgeoned. On the website for Shiloh Place, the healing ministry of Jack Frost, for example, I found some frightening statistics. Only one in forty currently active pastors will still be in ministry at the time of retirement. Some seventy percent of their adult children have sought clinical help for depression. Most pastors have considered quitting at some point in the last year.

An article in a Strang publication I read a few years ago echoes such statistics. It stated that every month, one thousand pastors in America leave the ministry permanently. Criticism, accusation and rampant lovelessness wear them down until despair and depression win out. Many pastors bring this kind of thing on themselves by their un-Christlike treatment of their people or by their ungodly responses to the everyday sins of those they lead. Pastors are as broken and human as anyone else, so the wounding cuts both ways—leadership and people hurting one another. Either way the root is lovelessness in the Church.

Are we not becoming ever more like the people Paul described in 2 Timothy? No other fruit could possibly come from the demonically inspired culture of self that we have allowed to invade our churches and our lives as Christians.

But Paul was only expanding on the words of Jesus:

"For nation will rise against nation, and kingdom against kingdom, and in various places there will be famines and earthquakes. But all these things are merely the beginning of birth pangs. Then they will deliver you to tribulation, and will kill you, and you will be hated by all nations because of My name."

Matthew 24:7–9

It would be difficult to argue that we do not see such things as famines, earthquakes and wars accelerating in the world around us. The number of wars, for example, fought in various parts of the world since World War II staggers the imagination. The United States alone has fought at least eight of them—Korea, Vietnam, Panama, Grenada, Kosovo, Afghanistan and two in Iraq! There have been civil wars, rebellions, wars between nations and ethnic conflicts. More Christians have been martyred in the last decade and a half than in all the previous history of the Church combined. All of these were and are manifestations of the rising tide of hatred. That being said, even though the signs are sobering, I refuse to fall in among those who predict with certainty the imminent return of Christ and the end of the world.

More sobering is the spiritual and moral condition of the Church, especially in the West. In my own city of Denver, Colorado, tens of thousands of people who used to attend church have drifted away, too often through simple disillusionment resulting from leadership failures, church splits and loss of true biblical purpose—all failures of love. Many still call themselves Christian, but in reality they espouse a hodgepodge of doctrines drawn from multiple sources, both Christian and non-Christian.

"Many false prophets will arise and will mislead many" (Matthew 24:11). False or impure prophecy runs rampant in the land. Witness the Y2K predictions I discussed in chapter 1. Another example is a well-substantiated prophecy of nuclear disaster that was to befall a major American city on March 3, 2003. A million and a half people were to die. Obviously this never came to pass. Such false prophecies are one more fruit of the arrogance Paul wrote about to Timothy.

Matthew 24:12 says, "Because lawlessness is increased, most people's love will grow cold." Moral relativism has become the cultural standard as the culture of self has taught us to become a law unto ourselves. Lawlessness has become the most significant threat to the Church to arise in centuries. Lawlessness is the big one in my view.

Cold Love Equals Hate

"Most people's love will grow cold" (Matthew 24:12). If a thing cannot be clearly seen as a manifestation of love, then we must certainly see it as shades of hate.

101

Anti-Semitism rises in Europe once more. Racial tensions of all kinds proliferate around the globe. In every corner of the world, the seeds of conflict have been sown, watered and fertilized. Heartless terrorism spreads from nation to nation like a malignant cancer. As an American, I am acutely aware of a worldwide increase in hatred for my own country, particularly among Arabic peoples. No kind of diplomacy, international aid or appeasement can or will serve to abate the anger of the Arab world toward the West.

The demon behind the religion of Islam continues to actively incite most of the world's one billion Muslims to hate America, and specifically Christians. Working in concert with one another, the controlling demonic powers behind almost every other faith on earth increasingly incite members of those faiths to persecute us. In a great many cases, nations dominated by those faiths severely restrict or outlaw Christian witnessing and even the practice of Christianity. Vivid pictures of hatred.

The Cause: Lawlessness

Scripturally, the cause of this growing worldwide wave of hatred is lawlessness. The root of lawlessness is a focus on self at the expense of the good of the whole. When the heart of a society turns to self, self becomes law. We then thrust aside the laws of God to allow freedom for each "self" to live according to his or her own law. Fornication, for instance, becomes acceptable if the individual feels it to be right, as does lying under certain circumstances, or cheating and so on.

When the culture of the world agrees upon no God-given moral standards or laws of love as being universally absolute, then it becomes possible to fly airplanes into skyscrapers and to stone Christians to death in the streets. It becomes possible for Christians to divorce at the same rate as those in the world. Churches split. People begin to see God's house as the last place in the world to find love because love has grown cold. It grew cold because we refused God's law, finding all manner of excuse for pursuing our own principles at the expense of the Word of God. It is self-centered Baalism all over again!

Alongside Baal in the Old Testament is the god Molech, whom I believe to be Baal by another name. Israel sacrificed its children to Molech by fire. Likewise, our own culture sacrifices its unborn children on the altar of individual rights—the right of the self to determine morality without reference to the eternal law of God.

The whole law is fulfilled in two commandments: to love the Lord our God with all our hearts, minds, souls and strength, and to love our neighbors as ourselves. But we do not actually do it, so love dies, and we pay the price at every level of our lives. I am convinced that a major reason for the great apostasy at the end of the age will be lovelessness in the Church. Lovelessness results from lawlessness, while lawlessness comes from self-focus.

We have been commanded to let no unwholesome word come from our mouths but only those words that are good for edification of others as the moment may require. But speaking the truth in love has too often become a religious excuse to shred one another under cover.

We have been commanded to love our enemies, to return blessing for cursing, to love as we have been loved. But we have written our own laws, our own excuses for the list of people we believe we have religious license to hate, and we call it "discernment." Sometimes we even call it "prophetic."

We have been commanded to forgive others so that our Father will forgive us. But we continually choose to postpone or reject our Savior's command to forgive, and so love dies on the altar of self.

In truth we have written our own rules and called them God's. But the law of God stands as the objective expression and definition of His love. When we disobey or ignore that law (lawlessness), we pay the price in love grown cold. The penalty for sin—lawlessness—is death. Disobedience, then, kills love.

The Demon

This rising tide of hatred may be the one Jesus spoke of in Matthew 24, but if I am uncertain of the eschatological significance of this tide, I am firmly convinced of its demonic origins:

> Finally, be strong in the Lord and in the strength of His might. Put on the full armor of God, so that you will be able to stand firm against the schemes of the devil. For our struggle is not against flesh and blood, but against the rulers, against the powers, against the world forces of this darkness, against the spiritual forces of wickedness in the heavenly places.
>
> Ephesians 6:10–12

Paul, in the original Greek, painted a picture of a well-organized army, complete with commanders and established ranks leading right down to the garden-variety foot-soldier demon. This army works by carefully crafted schemes, or strategies to deceive, in order to bend the minds, hearts and spirits of men to a destructive course.

A ruling or commanding demon—often called a principality—works by influencing the thoughts of men and women in order to alter the collective mind—the ways that entire national, ethnic, racial and cultural groups of people think and feel. In this way, the demonic thinking, inspired by the principality, begins to feel right and natural. Thus inspired, the pressure of the surrounding culture insinuates these ungodly ideas into our system of thought and belief until even outrageous notions seem reasonable.

Examples abound. While a human fetus is clearly life and just as certainly human, for instance, it has now become culturally acceptable to destroy that life in the womb. This clear act of murder has become "reasonable" to the majority of our population. Another example is anti-Semitism, which grew to dominate Nazi Germany through the inspiration of a principality of hatred that influenced the whole nation by means of the culture it created. These things appear ludicrous when examined objectively and critically, but they are made to seem sensible to the collective mind through demonically inspired deception that bends the unprotected minds of men and women to think the way the demon thinks.

First and foremost, our adversary is a deceiver. He twists what is wrong to make it appear right and dresses hatred in the garments of love. For love of God, the terrorist kills his thousands. For love of God, we murder even our Christian brothers and sisters with our criticisms and judgments. But it all flows from the same source in a demonic and lawless principality that points us toward self-focus: Baal.

The Deception of Hatred: A Prophecy

Baal's pervasive culture of self will ebb and flow, but it will grow larger over time and by stages, as a long-term and carefully laid scheme unfolds. It generates forms of hatred that subtly insinuate themselves into the cultures of the nations until these forms of hatred are made to seem normal, right and even self-evident. This principality will not be satisfied with pitting nation against nation, race against race or faith against faith. If allowed, it will invade our homes, our relationships and our churches to cause them to hate, divide and destroy—often in the name of the Lord.

It will insinuate itself into every undealt-with place of sin, insecurity, ambition, offense or judgment. It will energize every unsurrendered pocket of bitterness. It will fill and use any region of our lives in which we have not chosen mercy and sought the cross of Christ to crucify that which is not His heart. It will find and activate every place in us where we have not invited the Holy Spirit of God to come and rule by the blood of Jesus, which cleanses us from all sin and focuses us on the welfare of others beyond ourselves. For those unprotected by the presence of Jesus and for those believers whose unhealed hearts open the doors of their lives to demonic access, demonic hatred will seem both right and justified.

In the Church, it may take the form of trumped-up charges against pastors and one another. To those caught up in it, the charges will seem valid, their outrage justified. Once formed, these judgments become the filter through which to interpret every action of the one being judged. What was green to the one being judged now becomes brown to his or her accusers as they see it through their yellow filter. Brown is not the truth, but they can see it no other way because they are blind to the demonic filter they have adopted. Hatred results, cloaked in religious language and holy justification. This hatred is a demonic viciousness born of lawlessness that is ultimately derived from a relentless cultural emphasis on the rights and the centrality of self.

Matthew 18:15 admonishes believers to a process of confrontation and communication that would resolve most of this kind of internal conflict, but this process is seldom followed in the Church today. Even better, we could simply ask questions about what was meant by this or that and accept the answers we receive, but religious pride in our exalted discernment too seldom permits such humility. Self-focus. Lawlessness. Love grows cold.

This rising tide of hatred will destroy marriages, friendships, children, families and churches at an accelerating pace, and it will seem proper and normal to those caught up in it because they have been taught that the welfare of self is what life is all about. We are carried along by our hatreds, judgments and offenses because they seem justified. Too often we even believe these things come from God. If the enemy could not put a supernatural stamp on these things, we who claim the name of Jesus would never fall for the deception. The world just goes along with it all, but we believers tend to find ways to call it holy.

The deception of hatred says, "You were treated unfairly. You were wounded. You were insulted. You were discriminated against. You were belittled. You were abused. You have a right." This is self-focus, accessed and used! We all struggle with it. In this way, the spirit of hatred, the spirit of war, will come down from the collective level of the nations to deceive the individual on an individual basis.

Speaking the Truth in Love

As I have preached this message publicly and called for radical love among God's people, someone always protests, "But what about speaking the truth in love?" An important concept, I agree, but listen carefully: If we in the Body of Christ had really learned how to love, we would be ready and qualified to speak the truth in love, but as things stand, speaking the truth in love is too often nothing more than a cover for forms of verbal brutality that flow from a lack of love.

We are not ready to speak the truth in love until we understand love in the first place. But when it comes to understanding love, we are just beginners. Besides, the context of speaking the truth in love, as presented in Ephesians 4, has little or nothing to do with confrontation of the truth of one another's flaws. Ephesians 4:15 commands us to speak the truth to one another about Jesus, not about our human ugliness. The truth about Jesus would be an edifying and encouraging gift of love, would it not?

> I gave you milk to drink, not solid food; for you were not yet able to receive it. Indeed, even now you are not yet able, for you are still fleshly. For since there is jealousy and strife among you, are you not fleshly, and are you not walking like mere men?
>
> 1 Corinthians 3:2–3

I cannot count the times I have fallen into attempting to control the behavior of messy people under my care in the name of speaking the truth in love. It is my confession, not my accusation of anyone, that we are still too fleshly in the Body of Christ, in spite of decades of renewal. We have yet to plumb the depths of love, and until we have done that, where perceived sin is concerned we cannot speak the truth in love and have it actually be love. Prophetic confrontation may be the exception to my rule here, but truly prophetic people have had arrogance and the agenda of self cleansed out of them by the hand of God in crushing, humbling and death to self. Brokenness and sin can be confronted only in truly selfless love by those who have themselves been broken.

The Falling Away

Matthew 24:10 says many will fall away in the season preceding the return of the Lord. The cause of that great apostasy will be twofold as it flows from its root in hatred. Persecution will come from outside the Body of Christ, while excuses to hate will arise from inside.

This internal hate will flow from judgments, fears and loss of faith built up toward one another and toward God over the years, in part because we have been fed a prosperity doctrine of self that told us it was our inalienable right to prosper and feel good—that this was what becoming a believer was about. Those who offend against this perceived "right" then become worthy of our "loving" confrontation.

In the culture in which we have lived, love works for us when it feels good to love. We love because it benefits us to love, but the cross of Jesus teaches that love is truly love only when it costs us something.

Learning the Joy of Selflessness

Love cost Jesus everything. He had every right to call down ten legions of angels to avenge the injustice done to Him, but He chose to bear it for the sake of the very ones who were putting Him to death. In doing so, He taught us the true meaning of love: selflessness.

Love must always be the highest and greatest joy of true disciples, but in the days to come, we will find it both rare and costly. Those who choose genuine love will be swimming against the stream, and it will exact a price. As we pay that price, we are going to grow up, and we are going to begin to look a lot like Jesus.

This will, therefore, be our finest hour—the hour of promise. Even in the face of the great apostasy, this will

109

be the time when true believers emerge to conquer in love in the face of every kind of hatred and offense. This will be the test of whether or not we have understood the Gospel at all.

As we learn the true definition of love and our lives begin to be transformed to the image of Christ, the fruit will be evident: "But the one who endures to the end, he will be saved. This gospel of the kingdom shall be preached in the whole world as a testimony to all the nations, and then the end will come" (Matthew 24:13–14).

For the first time in history, the task of reaching every people group on the planet can be achieved in our lifetime. We know where they are, who they are and how to reach them. It can be done, and I believe we should expect that it will be done as true believers emerge to conquer in love. Mission agencies the world over are developing strategies and carrying them out as I write. When the task reaches completion, Jesus will return.

But even as the nations hear the Gospel, evil rises alongside. It is a good day to learn the joy of selflessness.

For all these reasons, I plead with you not to surrender to the wave of hatred! In the face of it, overcome evil with good. Study the cross until it captivates every aspect of your character. In the process, the precious will be separated from the vile, the genuine distinguished from the counterfeit.

Determine now to walk in the character of Jesus no matter what it may cost or where it may lead, else the rising tsunami wave of hatred about to engulf the world will sweep away and destroy all that you have and all that you are.

7

The Spirit of Independence and Rebellion

A driving force behind the culture of self that rules the Western world—particularly America—is the spirit of rebellion and independence. It subverts our spirituality, undermines our sense of the Father's love, defiles the exercise of our gifts and dulls our sense of the flow of God's power. With its focus on the exaltation of self, it falsely equates submission with being diminished, obedience with loss of freedom and servanthood with insignificance, blinding us to the gift of love that submission truly is.

The opposite Spirit, the remedy for rebellion and independence, is the Holy Spirit—the Spirit of Jesus, with His submissive and humble heart in subjection to His Father. With humble obedience as a settled element of His character, Jesus rose from the waters of the Jordan on the day of His baptism to hear the Father proclaim, "My beloved Son, in whom I am well-pleased" (Matthew 3:17). In other words, the Father saw His own heart reflected back to Him in His Son. It is as if He cried with pleasure, "That's My boy!" When God looks into a man, woman or congregation and sees His own heart reflected back to Him in the character of the person or people, He takes pleasure and delight in the same way He took pleasure and delight in Jesus.

A submissive heart makes three things possible: intimacy with the Father, power for miracles and love for people. God will grant us great things in the days to come, not because of the scintillating wonder of our programs or the perfection of our performance, but because He sees in us the imprint of the heart of His Son. That heart does only what it sees the Father doing and speaks only what it hears the Father speaking. It is the pure model of loving obedience.

Every Man Did What Was Right in His Own Eyes

Judges 17:6 describes the spirit in Israel prior to the kings: "In those days there was no king in Israel; every man did what was right in his own eyes." Because the people lived under no acknowledged authority, every man thought and did whatever he wanted to think and do, much as our own Western culture teaches us to do. In fact, independence and refusal to submit have become points of pride with us.

Judges 17 and 18 tell the story of Micah, who constructed a very expensive idol. Having done so, he hired a Levite as his private priest, believing that the presence of the priest would legitimize what he had done and bring the Lord's blessing. I find it revealing that the priest worked for Micah, rather than for God. In the spirit of independence, Micah formulated his own plan, not God's, and then expected God to back him up: "Now I know that the LORD will prosper me, seeing I have a Levite as priest" (Judges 17:13).

The men of the tribe of Dan saw what Micah had done (see chapter 18). Armed, they came and took away his hired priest and the idol he had made. Micah called his neighbors to ride with him, and when they overtook the Danites, the army asked Micah why he was pursuing them. Micah replied:

> "You have taken away my gods which I made, and the priest, and have gone away, and what do I have besides? So how can you say to me, 'What is the matter with you?'" The sons of Dan said to him, "Do not let your voice be heard among us, or else fierce men will fall upon you and you will lose your life, with the lives of your household." So the sons of Dan went on their way; and when Micah saw that they were too strong for him, he turned and went back to his house.
>
> Judges 18:24–26

In Micah's system of belief, loss of the priest meant loss of the Lord's favor, presence and anointing, together with the material prosperity he believed it would bring. Micah lost everything he thought he had.

All this came about because self stood at the center, unsubmitted and independent, every man doing what was right in his own eyes. Because Micah's plan was not the Lord's, it failed.

In the independent spirit that is unsubmitted to God's legitimate authority—as represented in a king, priest, pastor or other appointed figure—the Lord's plan can never take shape. Nothing can come from the spirit of independence and rebellion except the failed plans of men, loss of the presence of God at a spiritual level and poverty at an economic level. God sees rebellion against His appointed authority as rebellion against Himself. The root of Adam's sin—and of every trespass committed thereafter—is the spirit of rebellion and independence that causes one to believe he or she can somehow do better than God. Then when things do not go as well as one plans, he or she blames God and wonders why the plan went awry. This is what happened to Micah. We must cultivate a heart of healthy respect and submission to whatever authority God has placed in our lives, wherever He has placed it.

Grumbling against God's Chosen Leadership

Miriam and Aaron served as two of Moses' most important lieutenants as he led the people of Israel out of slavery.

> Miriam and Aaron spoke against Moses because of the Cushite woman whom he had married . . . and they said, "Has the LORD indeed spoken only through Moses? Has He not spoken through us as well?" And the LORD heard it.
>
> Numbers 12:1–2

Miriam and Aaron took offense at a personal decision Moses made in choosing to marry a woman of whom they disapproved, and they used this judgment to justify self-exaltation at Moses' expense.

Grumbling against God's chosen leadership has always been one of the most revealing and consistent manifestations of the spirit of rebellion and independence. If the enemy can destroy or weaken God's appointed structures of authority and order, then he can destroy God's people. Self-focus breeds self-importance, which consistently goes hand in hand with rebellion. Self rises up in arrogance to take offense at the favor given to others, especially to those in authority.

Angry at what He regarded as an affront to Himself, the Lord struck Miriam with leprosy, separating her from her people. The spirit of rebellion and independence removes a person from the protection of the authority structure God appointed for him or her, and it is a frequent underlying cause of physical illness. In my observation, common manifestations are cancer and chronic maladies of various kinds.

Those ensnared by the spirit of rebellion and independence almost always justify themselves on the basis of distortion or misapplication of godly truth. Of course Aaron and Miriam heard from God! But that did not make them Moses' peers. God had given Moses a position of authority and leadership that He had not given them. For His own sake He expected that position to be respected. Because God Himself had appointed Moses to this position of leadership, their rebellion stood as an affront to His own honor.

The Rebellion of Korah

In Numbers 16, Israel is still in the wilderness, having fled Egypt and slavery. Infected with the same spirit of rebellion that afflicted Aaron and Miriam, Korah rose up against Moses. But unlike Miriam and Aaron, he recruited others to stand with him.

> They assembled together against Moses and Aaron, and said to them, "You have gone far enough, for all the congregation are holy, every one of them, and the LORD is in their

midst; so why do you exalt yourselves above the assembly of the LORD?"

verse 3

Nearly fifteen thousand people died in the wrath of God that fell in response to Korah's offense. Because Miriam and Aaron kept their rebellion to themselves, the penalty for their sin was limited to Miriam's leprosy, which the Lord quickly removed in response to their repentance and Moses' prayer. Korah actively enlisted others, spreading his rebellion through the camp. His arrogant divisiveness, therefore, brought more than temporary illness. People died.

Korah made his rebellion sound so theologically correct, so righteous—as do so many people today. "We are all holy. We are all equals. See how arrogant this man Moses is?" True—all God's people are holy, but again, God had appointed Moses to a position, and with it He bestowed authority to act in His name before the people. That position did not make him superior to anyone. It was simply the office God gave him.

When the people of God grant respect to a man or woman in authority for the sake of the position he or she holds and as an act of love for the person and for the Lord, the Father sees the heart of His Son reflected back to Him. In response, God releases blessing in the same way He released blessing on Jesus when He cried out His pleasure that day at the Jordan River. The culture of self, inspired by the demon Baal, seeks to prevent all this by exalting self to a position not appointed for self to hold.

My Own Test of Honor

In 1977, I was just a year out of seminary and very young. The senior pastor who had hired me as his youth

116

director was moved to another parish, and denominational authorities assigned another to take his place. The new man arrived a little blinded by his past position of influence, success and respect, and began making changes without taking time to listen to the people for a sense of who they were and where they had been. A common and understandable error!

An experienced former leader of youth, he began asking for changes in my youth group that would have destroyed it had I carried them out. His suggestions would have made sense in any other setting, but this group's history was a bit unique. He was not listening and did not realize what he was missing.

Soon a line of church members beat a path to my door to complain. Some spoke of going to the district office to have this man removed. Young and out of my depth, I was miserable and in danger of being swept up in the rising tide of criticism, not to mention my swelling sense of self-importance.

At the point of sharpest crisis, an invitation to lunch came from a seasoned pastor who was part of the same denomination in a neighboring community and who had learned of the situation. Gently, but firmly, he confronted me with two of the most significant truths I had heard up until that point in my young life. Reminding me of the story of David and Saul, he challenged me to be my senior pastor's support and advocate and gave warning that my treatment of this man would determine the way my own subordinates would relate to me when I became a senior pastor myself. Humbled, chastened and newly possessed of a smaller hat size, I nodded my head in understanding and then followed him to my knees by the couch, where we prayed.

In the weeks that followed, I became my senior pastor's advocate with the wider congregation. Individually I decided to honor him with my trust by speaking the truth openly concerning what would happen if I made the changes he was asking for in my youth program. I quickly learned that I had been blind—that he was a team player and had wanted this from me all along. In the months that followed, he settled in as the fine pastor he really was, beloved of his people and a good mentor for me.

Whether that man was right or wrong was never really the issue. That kind of questioning leads only to judgment. The real issue on God's heart was whether or not I would be willing to honor the man in self-sacrificial love for the sake of the heart of Jesus. My choices helped free that good servant to show us all God had deposited in him for our benefit.

Penalties and Reapings

As the stories from the Old Testament illustrate, rebellion against the Lord's anointed can bring sickness and sometimes death. Does that apply today? I have often said that we would one day see the days of Ananias and Sapphira return to the Church, times when the flow of the Lord's power and anointing would be so strong that violations of it could result in physical death. Within the last four years I have seen both sickness and death occur at least four times as the clear result of rebellion and of leveling reviling accusations at Church authority. Really! People died! In these four cases, illness and death descended in ways dramatic enough that only a fool would fail to notice.

It did not matter that the targeted leaders might have been truly guilty of the character flaws the critics pointed out. What mattered was that these people recruited others into rebellion as Korah did and died long before their time.

Let's be clear. We do not serve a God of domination or control, but rather a God of authority. At issue in these stories from the time of Moses is not whether Moses was right, wrong, humble or prideful. At issue was the position Moses held that had to be respected in selfless love for the Lord's sake. I do not believe God objected to anyone's having a disagreement with His designated leadership. What mattered to God then and now is the way those in disagreement carry themselves. How might the outcome have been different had Miriam, Aaron and even Korah humbly said, "Moses, we think we have heard from God concerning these issues of disagreement. We submit these things to you. We leave it in your hands to decide what to do." God took issue not with disagreement, but with dishonor and open rebellion.

My Congregation Started with Rebellion

My current congregation came together with rebellion at its heart. For long and terrible years we struggled with strife and division. As a result, we could not grow. One of the most significant root causes of our failure was the determination of virtually every leader and layperson in the church to do whatever he or she thought was right in his or her own eyes. Group leaders refused our training and rejected the resources we provided for study, insisting on following their own courses. And then they wondered why they failed.

In contrast, our current leaders follow the guidelines, using our study materials and listening to counsel. Because God has established a healthy spirit of submission and respect, our current leaders succeed where the former crop failed. Where pastoral staff members once walked in rebellion, quarreling with me regarding our values and the application of them and seeing little anointing on their ministries, I now have cooperation and honor. As a result, each of my current staff members now sees his or her ministry blessed with expansion and anointing. God is the same yesterday and forever, and His principles reflect that same consistency, even three and four thousand years later.

This is not a chapter on servant leadership, but it must be said that I value servant leadership and categorically reject any and all forms of domination and control. Authority does not translate into control. Any leader who must control the people he or she leads never had the authority to begin with. Prosperity and blessing come when a leader leads as Jesus led and when the people follow with humility and respect, speaking the truth in love. I cannot say that I always lead that way—some of my mistakes are legendary—but I can say that I long to lead that way and that I want to know when and why I have failed.

The Penalties of Rebellion

According to the scriptural record, seven penalties result from rebellion and independence. We find the first three in the stories of Micah, Aaron and Miriam, and Korah:

1. Material poverty
2. Sickness, often chronic
3. Death

The next three penalties can be found in 1 Samuel 15. Samuel, as the representative of the Lord, instructed Saul concerning the spoil taken from the Amalekites, whom they were about to defeat in battle. Every bit of it was to be given to the Lord in sacrifice and utterly destroyed. But Saul compromised, allowing some of it to be kept for sacrifice later, in his own way at his own time.

> Samuel said,
> "Has the LORD as much delight in burnt offerings and
>   sacrifices
> As in obeying the voice of the LORD?
> Behold, to obey is better than sacrifice,
> And to heed than the fat of rams.
> For rebellion is as the sin of divination,
> And insubordination is as iniquity and idolatry.
> Because you have rejected the word of the LORD,
> He has also rejected you from being king."
>
> 1 Samuel 15:22–23

Saul's rebellion led to the fourth biblical penalty of rebellion and independence:

4. Loss of anointing and authority

So Saul complained that the people made him do it. It was not his fault! Circumstances dictated his actions! Instead of walking in power and dignity, Saul became a victim. The opposite of walking in authority is to live as a powerless victim. Never able to own his own sin, Saul claimed always to be the victim of circumstances. Rampant self-focus robs us of the ability to take personal responsibility for failure.

At heart, Saul clung to simple rebellion. Because of this rebellion written so deeply into his character, God took authority from Saul and gave it to David. He could look to David, see His own heart there in godly submission and cry out, "That's my boy!"

"Now the Spirit of the LORD departed from Saul, and an evil spirit from the LORD terrorized him" (1 Samuel 16:14). As a result of his rebellion and independence, then, Saul suffered the next two penalties on the list:

5. Depression and insanity
6. Loss of the sense of God's presence

Insanity and loss of the Lord's presence affected not only Saul himself but also his household. Saul's own son, Jonathan, fled the ravages of his father's depravity, and so they lived estranged. Rebellion and independence give legal permission to the enemy of our souls to kill, steal and destroy.

At the point of the beginning of rebellion, spiritual and emotional maturation cease in the area of that rebellion. This leads to the final biblical penalty of rebellion and independence:

7. Immaturity

Many unchurched Christians, for example, reject the authority represented by any local body of believers and wander in rebellion. Without exception I see and grieve that such believers fail to truly grow beyond the point of their maturity at the beginning of their rebellion. And unless they repent, rejoin a fellowship and determine to set personal offense aside for the sake of love, they will never grow again.

Although my parents are so widely known for healing and wisdom, they once were foolish young people just like the rest of us. As their firstborn, I became the experimental child. In those early days my father accepted the philosophy so popular at the time that the purpose of discipline was to break a child's will. The fact that I was exceptionally strong-willed therefore made an eventual collision inevitable.

I could not have been more than four or five years old when it came. I do not even remember what act of reckless disobedience triggered the incident, but I clearly remember the outcome. To break my will by means of humiliation, my parents placed a bowl of beans on one side of the room and an empty bowl on the other. I was forced to take a bean from one bowl and push it across the hardwood floor with my nose to the other bowl, all the while reciting, "I will obey, I will obey, I will obey," one bean at a time until the bowl was empty. Outwardly I complied, but my heart rose up in angry rebellion to vow, "I will never obey!"

At that point, my capacity for selfless love in a gift of submission immediately ceased to grow. As a result I lived the better part of the next four decades stuck in immaturity in a hidden part of my emotional life that made it difficult for me to submit inwardly to any form of authority. I grew up, became a man and did manly and honorable things, but my growth had been stunted in that hidden place at the point of the beginning of rebellion.

Outwardly in the mature part of me, the grown man preached submission and willingly rendered honor to those over him as best he could. But inwardly, turmoil and struggle prevented the grown-up from learning much that he could have learned from those to whom he could have submitted, had he been able. Much unnecessary loneliness followed until finally, on the counseling couch, revelation came, repentance followed and freedom grew.

Ability to submit to authority as a selfless sacrifice in love for the sake of the welfare of others stands as a certain indicator of maturity. In the military, for example, one cannot be regarded as a grown-up until he or she can take orders. One who cannot obey can never be mature. Similarly, we regard children to be growing in maturity when they learn to obey willingly.

In his rebellion, Saul remained a spiritual child, unstable and unfit to reign until the day he died. God passed the kingdom to David—who, in point of fact, committed much worse sins than Saul—but David was a grown-up who could submit to the word of the prophet when necessary and own his own sin. Where there is no submission, there can be no maturity, and where there is no maturity, there can be no authority.

David's Heart of Honor

David's capacity for godly submission and honor stood up under fire. As Saul fell into insanity and David's popularity grew, Saul began seeking to eliminate him. Two stories reveal clearly why God granted the kingdom to David, rather than Saul, and why at the end of David's life God called him a man after His own heart.

When Saul hunted David with an army of several thousand men, David hid in a cave (see 1 Samuel 24). Into that very cave came Saul to relieve himself. Hiding there in the darkness, David's men urged him in low whispers,

> "Behold, this is the day of which the LORD said to you, 'Behold; I am about to give your enemy into your hand, and you shall do to him as it seems good to you.'" Then David arose and cut off the edge of Saul's robe secretly. It came about afterward that David's conscience bothered him because he had cut off the edge of Saul's robe.

> verses 4–5

124

David, a man after God's own heart, understood the principles behind self-sacrificing submission and honor.

> So he said to his men, "Far be it from me because of the LORD that I should do this thing to my lord, the LORD's anointed, to stretch out my hand against him, since he is the LORD's anointed." David persuaded his men with these words and did not allow them to rise up against Saul.
>
> verses 6–7

David honored and led others to honor.

God saw His own nature reflected in David, in a heart for honor and godly submission as he rendered the gift of love to Saul, to the Lord and to his people. It was a sacrifice of self that meant David's own suffering and persecution would continue for a time. In that attitude David prospered, while Saul died broken and insane.

In 1 Samuel 26, Saul again was hunting David. Accompanied by a lieutenant named Abishai, David stole into Saul's camp by night and entered his tent.

> Then Abishai said to David, "Today God has delivered your enemy into your hand; now therefore, please let me strike him with the spear to the ground with one stroke, and I will not strike him the second time." But David said to Abishai, "Do not destroy him, for who can stretch out his hand against the LORD's anointed and be without guilt? . . . The LORD forbid that I should stretch out my hand against the LORD's anointed."
>
> verses 8–9, 11

Once more God saw His own heart reflected in David. David, the obedient. David, the worshipper. David, who knew the presence of God. David, the writer of psalms. David, pursuer of God. David, blessed of the Lord. David, so full of the gift of authority from God that he united the divided tribes of Israel and made them powerful in the earth.

The Submissive Heart of Jesus

These principles applied to Jesus in the same way they apply to us. Luke 2:51–52 summarizes the years after His *bar mitzvah* in Jerusalem, the time when His culture declared Him a man under God, a son of the covenant: "He continued in subjection to [Mary and Joseph]. . . . And Jesus kept increasing in wisdom and stature, and in favor with God and men."

Note the direct connection between submission to His earthly parents in love and the favor He received both from His heavenly Father and from all the people who knew Him. Healthy submission to those whom God places in authority releases favor and honor on those who render it. If it held true for Jesus, it must certainly be so for us. But self-focus and the religion of Baal rob us of this blessing.

Matthew 3 describes how the grown Jesus, the Son of the living God, humbly submitted to John the Baptist for baptism—John, to whom no miracle of any kind or outward demonstration of power was ever attributed. Later Jesus asserted repeatedly, "I do only what I see My Father doing and say only what I hear My Father saying" (paraphrased). He subjected Himself both to men and to His Father for the sake of loving His Father. Submission.

Being found in appearance as a man, He humbled Himself by becoming obedient to the point of death, even death on a cross. For this reason also, God highly exalted Him, and bestowed on Him the name which is above every name, so that at the name of Jesus EVERY KNEE WILL BOW.

Philippians 2:8–10

126

For Jesus, healthy submission to His Father's authority led to exaltation and the gift of authority.

The same holds true for you and me, in that God gives honor, position and authority to wield His power and blessing for prosperity and favor. But He must see in us a heart of obedience and healthy submission offered in selfless love, both to Him directly and to the human authority He has placed in our lives—whether it is a group leader at church, a ministry director or pastor, the boss at work, a husband or a wife. This is one essential key to our dreams, our hope of prosperity, our authority and our intimacy with God. Let not the culture of self teach us that exaltation comes from the advancement of self at the expense of those the Lord has placed in authority over us.

8

The Birthright of Freedom
and Grace

———————•———————

I have written this book not to condemn or lay burdens on tired saints, but to set us free from the heaviness of a demonically inspired system that has robbed us of our birthright in Christ by insinuating lies and deceptions into our faith, values and belief systems. Isn't it time for us to claim the real birthright in all its glory and to move rest-fully and powerfully into all the Lord has held in reserve for us as a people and as a Church? Isn't it time to reject the lie that if I do not fight for "mine," then I will not have what is "mine"? And that if I live a life of sacrifice, it will wear me out?

Living for self and interpreting the Scriptures in light of the agenda of self-fulfillment ultimately lead to method, striving, legalism and exhaustion. But selfless living leads to life, not loss. Really. *If* one lives by grace.

It is grace—not law—that saves us. The very first theological definition I learned when I came to Jesus was that grace means undeserved love. Undeserved. Love is received. Love is given. How can that be a burden?

In Matthew 10, Jesus Himself carefully instructed His disciples in the content and manner of the ministry they were to deliver on their first missionary journey. He sent them two by two to heal the sick, cast out demons and preach, blessing them with authority to do these things effectively. The most important instruction, couched in profound simplicity, is found in verse 8: "Freely you received, freely give." Freely. No restraint. No limitation. No bargaining with God or making deals like, "If you do this, I'll do that." It was not for the purpose of satisfying the disciples' own need for importance or position. It was simply, "Freely you received, freely give." The mission parameters pointed them beyond themselves in freedom and grace.

Later in Acts 2, the Holy Spirit fell on these same disciples in a new way. As the power overflowed them, they began giving away what they had received with such wonder and fervor that in the space of a single day the lives of three thousand people were forever touched, changed and saved. Thousands more followed in the ensuing weeks. The anointing—the love—flowed freely, easily and naturally from the infinite heart of God through His people.

From the beginning, the defining factor in the faith and practice of the apostles was to continue the dynamic of freely receiving grace—undeserved love—and then freely passing it on. I can think of no better antidote to the influence of the culture of self.

A Historical Perspective

History demonstrates that whenever the Holy Spirit has been poured out upon a people and the people allow Him to work freely rather than theologizing Him away or creating pseudo-scriptural behavioral rules to control how He works in, through and upon us, then God's people have experienced wonderful encounters with Jesus. Filled up with Him as a result of those experiences, they have gone out into the world to freely give because they have freely received.

Tragically, however, the Church's well-intentioned theologizers almost always intrude upon the free-flowing wonder of the outpouring of the Spirit to inform everyone what the rules must be. Instead of beginning with the free and wonderful experience of the Holy Spirit and then learning wisdom from the Scriptures to guide and govern that experience, the theologizers start with rules and then try to produce the experience—or squelch it. It never works.

This is what caused the demise of the charismatic renewal of the 1960s and 1970s. Revival always shipwrecks on the twin reefs of the service of self and the efforts of the theologizers to control it with rules and regulations.

In spiritual matters, as in life, form follows function. The biblical prophets and apostles first experienced God—the function—and then defined what they had experienced—the form—not the other way around. Scripture resulted. Form followed function. You and I must first be free to experience God, but then we must become disciplined enough to define and govern that experience by the scriptural record.

When we turn that process around by attempting to produce experience from rules, regulations and self-centered human control, revival inevitably dies. Legalism, devoid of the living and active presence of the Holy Spirit, is all that remains. The Church then enters that safe and secure place in the spirit of religion where God never does anything unexpected. He is under control. And so are we.

Okay, I will admit that was tongue-in-cheek. God can never be controlled. But when we try to control the movement of the Holy Spirit, we shield ourselves from entering into all that God longs to do in us as a Body.

The truth is that the moving of God's Spirit on the hearts of men and women has always produced disorder and always will. Absorption of the mess produced by revival seems to be the inevitable price we pay for receiving the goodness and blessing of life in Him.

Revival has always appeared outwardly to be disorderly and has therefore always generated controversy among the religious. In my own church, within a few months of the time when we began falling, shaking, laughing and being radically changed by the visitation of the Spirit, people we loved left us. We grieved, but the joy of the touch of God outweighed any grief we felt. We would choose the presence of God rather than the comfort of men over and over again. Equally certain, however, is the fact that what we have received freely from God in revival has moved us to freely and easily give it away.

But by the time the theologizers and rule-makers have finished, what was and should be a relationship of receiving and giving has become a religion of doing and performing focused on self and self-effort. God never intended that for us. It is the sort of Pharisaic religion Jesus so deeply despised and sought to undo. Weren't the Pharisees of Jesus' day the very paradigm of self-centered pride and self-righteousness?

Religion as doing and performing has failed everywhere it has been practiced. It will ever be so.

A friend of mine once said that a candy bar is only truly a candy bar when you simply eat it. You lose something essential when you separate the peanuts from the caramel, and the caramel from the chocolate. It just does not taste the same. Theologizers and rule-makers take the flavor and the fun out of the experience of knowing the Lord and freely giving His love away. It is best if we just innocently experience Him.

Historically, each time the Church has fallen away from freely experiencing and receiving the presence of the Lord and has adopted a doing and performing stance, four things have occurred: Revival has ended, the Church and its people have turned in on themselves, the stream of souls being saved has dried up and miracles have all but ceased. Spiritual and emotional exhaustion have followed, because it was the fire and fuel of the Spirit that kept the Church going. Without that fire, the fun dies and the Body becomes too tired to give anything away, to focus one another outward or to experience the joy of walking with the Lord. The theologizers call the doing and performing "maturity" and "stability," but Jesus calls it death.

Revivals always have been accompanied by the same disorder and the same messy manifestations, no matter where or when those revivals have broken out. But at the same time they have never failed to produce great missions movements and powerful social programs. The Holy Spirit is the Spirit of Jesus, and He carries the Master's selfless character. Consequently the world has been profoundly changed, fed and ministered to by historic revival movements. But by the time the theologizers and rule-makers finish their work, most of that ceases. The institutions remain, but the fun and fuel have been spent or drained away.

Ordinary believers and ministers then lose hope because they no longer see the kind of fruit for their labor that they saw when they were free to receive in the Holy Spirit and when their giving was powered by the wonder of His presence. In the face of such discouragement and lifelessness, many once zealous believers stop going to church at all. That is the cycle of history.

What Is Happening Now?

As I write, the Toronto Airport Christian Fellowship continues to enjoy an unabated outpouring of the Spirit of God that first broke out in January 1994. The same outpouring has affected my own church since 1996. It has been wonderful. For the first time in my life, church has been fun. Our congregation has been cleansed and healed. Lives have changed as never before. We have seen miracles and healings biblical in their proportion. A self-absorbed and sick people who once bit and devoured one another has become a loving, outreaching army of God that is affecting its community for good. The culture of self and the spirit that powers it have taken a significant beating in our midst as the Lord has made these changes.

Similar stories of transformation are being told all over the world. But in spite of all this, the Body of Christ in the West remains infected with the legacy of the years when the Church theologized away the working of the Holy Spirit—when legalism and rule keeping were the order of the day. This legacy of legalism seeped into Western church culture and insinuated itself into our belief system, crippling us. When coupled with the culture of self, the effect has been doubly deadly. In fact, legalism is really just another form of self-focus in both method and fruit, and therefore produces only death.

The Great Lie

It is as if someone held out to us a carrot on a stick and told us a great lie, promising something like: "If you could just do it right, work hard, get all your ducks in a row, then the blessing of God would flow in your life and you would have peace, prosperity and happiness."

That promise contained two major problems. One was the demand to perform in order to obtain blessing. The other was the self-focus inherent in the reason for doing it. Our attention slowly turned from freely receiving and then freely giving to a focus on what we ourselves must do, or what we ourselves needed and must perform in order to obtain what we needed.

When the culture of self goes religious, legalism and striving always result. It is a good thing, for example, to say the right things about Jesus—it is called praise. In this I can respect what the word-of-faith people have to say. But in too many places we Christians have turned praise into a new legalism. We have been told to "confess" this and "confess" that in order to obtain this or achieve that. We have been taught that God cannot bless us if we "confess" anything negative. Consequently we have begun to strive to speak all the right things and to avoid letting the wrong things come out of our mouths. In doing so, we have played directly into the hands of recycled Baalism, the cult of fertility and prosperity, that motivates our culture.

We labor at this form of religious "magic," but not only is it exhausting, it is also an exercise in futility. It is not about human striving to produce; it is about grace, mercy and favor. Freely you have received. Freely give.

Many of us transformed even God's loving gift of healing into a legalism. Healing mercy became something we labored to receive by performing all the right rituals, even if we did not call them rituals. If you received prayer but did not manifest a healing, it was because you did not have enough faith. So you were taught to strive to believe and to confess your healing, even if it did not manifest—or you were condemned for believing too little. The effort focused us inward, on ourselves, cutting off the dynamic of freely receiving so we could freely give.

We were told we had to have enough faith to get anything from God, as if five pounds of faith might produce five pounds of healing. In reality, fewer healings, not more, happened under this teaching because the economy of the Kingdom of God is simpler than that. Freely you have received. Freely give. The key word is "freely."

Where our marriages were concerned, instead of freely receiving the Lord's love and freely giving it to our spouses as that love transformed us and taught us selflessness, we began to look away from the sustaining power of the Holy Spirit to rely on new and wonderful teachings. The teachings were good; we needed them. But we turned them into a new legalism, centered in our own efforts and abilities instead of being sustained and energized by the Holy Spirit. And by their very nature, these forms of legalism focused us on ourselves and thereby stole our joy.

Even our hunger for revival has been infected with the spirit of striving. If all the churches could just attain unity, then Jesus would come in revival. And so, focused on ourselves and what we can do, we pastors labor, pray and heap meetings on top of meetings. We seek unity, desperately hoping to achieve enough of that mysterious state of oneness sufficient to convince God to send revival. This is futility!

The truth of revival unity is that Jesus first comes, we hear Him calling, and then we come to unity to give to one another what He is giving to us all. Unity does not produce revival. Rather, revival calls us to unity.

We have been told that if we would all just restructure our churches and become cell-based, herding everyone into small groups, then a long list of amazing things would happen. It does not work that way. First we receive the Spirit of God in power, as they did in Acts 2, and then He calls us joyfully into fellowship, breaking bread from house to house. Again, form must follow function.

Sometimes we think that if we could just get all our church systems functioning properly at the same time—from children and youth ministries to men's and women's groups, to ministry to the poor, to missions outreach—then God would bless us and we would grow. But at the beginning, the Church in Acts 2 had no functioning systems at all, and it grew to three thousand in one day. By God's Spirit, three thousand people almost immediately came to love one another deeply and sacrificially. It is all there in the biblical record. It happened because in the end it is not our ability to get it right that makes it all work. It is the grace, mercy and favor of the God who loves us.

Freely receiving. Freely giving. In that order.

The Spirit of Criticism

The Western church has come down with a terminal case of the spirit of criticism. The critical spirit arises out of the Pharisaic way of doing things and is an infallible indicator that we have fallen from grace into works and self-focus. Self-focus inevitably leads us to criticize those who will not or do not serve that focus. If we really believe the lie that we must get it all together and perform it all perfectly for God to love us and bless us, then we find ourselves compelled to be upset when those around us fail. According to legalistic thinking, human failure shuts down the blessing, and so we criticize and demand.

"The children's minister did not handle the children's ministry properly when that crisis happened. . . . The visitation team did not visit me in the hospital when I had that surgery. . . . The counseling director is a bit controlling. . . . The senior pastor is a little too aloof. . . . Isn't the director of the women's ministry a little pushy?"

We tear one another to shreds with our demands for performance based on our fear that God will not or cannot bless us through the barrier of human failure. And it is all fed by our self-focus, our need to be served rather than to serve. Don't we believe in the cross?

We have bought into the same performance lie that infected the Pharisees. It became a saying among the orthodox that if all Jewish people everywhere could obey the Law perfectly for just one day, then the Messiah would come. But the Kingdom of God is not about human performance. It is about the grace and mercy of God who loves us and blesses us because He is good, not because we are good. He blesses because He is righteous, not because we humans have achieved His blessing. He blesses us because He Himself has done it right, not because we sinners got it done. He is God; we are not. That is why He blesses!

Jesus did not tell His disciples, "Wonderfully you have performed; now wonderfully give." Revival is *all* about freely receiving from Jesus and then freely giving what we have freely received. To receive is an experience—not a theology, idea or principle. To give it away is a demonstration that we truly understand what we have experienced and why we were blessed with it.

Grace in the Bible

The Scriptures abound with examples of God's grace— grace that redeems us, grace that delivers us, grace that brings anointing and opens the door to all good things of the Lord. Regardless of our sin and imperfections, the grace of God freely poured out for us overcomes it all—if only we will receive Him.

Romans

In Romans 7 and 8, Paul bemoans his apparent helplessness before the onslaught of his personal sin and celebrates the grace of Jesus who delivered him from it:

> And we know that God causes all things to work together for good to those who love God, to those who are called according to His purpose. . . . What then shall we say to these things? If God is for us, who is against us? He who did not spare His own Son, but delivered Him over for us all, how will He not also with Him freely give us all things? . . . For I am convinced that neither death, nor life, nor angels, nor principalities, nor things present, nor things to come, nor powers, nor height, nor depth, nor any other created thing, will be able to separate us from the love of God, which is in Christ Jesus our Lord.
>
> Romans 8:28, 31–32, 38–39

In Christ, God's transforming love comes free of charge and cannot be taken from us.

Corinth

The biblical record shows us an exceedingly messy congregation in Corinth that was doing just about everything wrong. According to 1 Corinthians 11, for instance, a number of wealthy people, absorbed in self and self-importance, ignored the poor and seemed proud of it, eating of their own abundance during the fellowship meals that were part of the celebration of the Lord's Supper while the poor and hungry looked on.

Furthermore, in their self-absorption they abused the gifts of the Spirit, wearing them as badges of rank and pride. They exercised the gift of tongues chaotically and abused the prophetic word.

Factions vied with one another for dominance and position as they identified with Apollos or with Paul, rather than with the Lord, as they should have. One man in Corinth (see chapter 5) fell so deeply into depravity that Paul actually decided to turn him over to Satan for discipline, stating his dismay that the church did not seem upset by the presence of this heinous sin in their midst.

But here is the wonderful part: In spite of its imperfections, next to the church in Jerusalem as described in Acts 2, the church in Corinth was easily the most vibrant and exciting congregation in the New Testament. Human performance will not and cannot produce anointing. Anointing is the grace, mercy and favor of God freely given.

David

God blessed King David so much that he became Israel's greatest king. I have already pointed out how he united the tribes and defeated their enemies. The Father Himself deemed David a man after God's own heart whose lineage produced Jesus the Messiah. And God did all of this for David in spite of his adultery with Bathsheba and the murder of her husband, Uriah. The open secret is that David knew how to humbly repent. David was also a worshipper who loved the Lord with all his heart. In the face of failure, therefore, God gave grace. Freely receiving. Freely giving.

Peter

The apostle Peter—a mess if ever there was one—denied the Lord three times on the eve of the crucifixion, met the risen Christ and then illegally abandoned the ministry to return to fishing (see John 21). In that culture, when a man received a call to follow after a prophet, he was to leave his old life and never return. This is why Elisha destroyed his oxen and implements for plowing when Elijah called him. He was burning his bridges to the old way. In the New Testament, Jesus admonished the disciples that one who puts his hand to the plow and looks back is not fit for the Kingdom. Same principle.

Having once been called, Peter's old life as a fisherman had become illegal. When Jesus found Peter fishing again—his old profession—He challenged him three times whether or not he loved Him and three times commanded him to feed His sheep. In that culture, to ask once was acceptable, twice constituted an insult, and to ask the same question a third time was a backhanded slap in the face. So Peter was deeply grieved at the repeated questioning. Jesus used a radical form of shock therapy to drive home the point that Peter had been called to feed the sheep and could never return to the old way of making a living.

So Peter had failed significantly—not once, but twice. Yet Jesus filled him with power and set him over the church in Jerusalem. Thousands came to the Lord through him and were filled with the Spirit at his hands. Freely you have received. Freely give. And Peter did choose to give!

Later he went to Antioch, where he fell under the influence of the Judaizers (see Galatians 2:11) and refused to eat with the Gentile believers. Paul was forced to rebuke him openly. A failure once more! Yet Jesus loved him and kept giving him the Spirit. He ended up evangelizing in the city of Rome, capital of the empire, choosing to give what he had freely received, rather than continue in any form of self-focus. Our walk is not about the self-focus that lies at the heart of human performance. It is the grace and mercy of God. The only thing Peter needed was to love the Lord with all his strength, to keep a repentant heart before God and to keep giving what he had been given.

"The sacrifices of God are a broken spirit; a broken and a contrite heart, O God, You will not despise. By Your favor do good to Zion; build the walls of Jerusalem" (Psalm 51:17–18). It is a humility issue, isn't it? It is by His favor that the walls are built, not by human power or human goodness.

What Is Needed Now?

What is needed in order for us to truly live the New Testament, to do the works of Jesus and greater works than He did, as He promised? Must we pray hard enough? Long enough? Is there some mysterious threshold of numbers beyond which an intercessory prayer meeting becomes effective before God? Is it that we must all share the proper attitude? How much repentance is enough repentance? Does God require that each of us conquer all our vices in order to be blessed? Maybe if none of us ever fought with or judged one another?

Or is it still about freely receiving and freely giving? The grace and favor of God are our life and strength. Be a lover of God. Be a worshipper. Have a repentant, humble and broken heart before God. Receive the love Father God has for you, and then keep receiving it. Be willing and active in the work of giving it away. These are the qualifiers. This is the Gospel! In it God gets the glory, rather than the pitiful humans who try to manage what He is doing or call down His presence by their own effort.

Jesus invited us to take His yoke upon us as something easy and light, in contrast to the man-made burden the Pharisees imposed. He called us to come to Him and He would give us rest. Freely we have received.

Toward the end of the charismatic renewal in the 1980s, I learned a little song that went like this:

Mary had a little lamb that never became a sheep.
It became a charismatic and died from lack of sleep.

We just didn't get it, did we? Starting with the Spirit of God, we ended with a load of burdens that led us inevitably to self-focus. That self-focus has now stolen the hope and fire from huge numbers of us.

I myself got caught up in trying to reveal and heal enough of my personal bitter roots so that I would at last be happy and worthy of blessing. It became a new and dead self-centered legalism to which I finally called an end until I could find the balance in grace. Eventually I did keep seeking healing and submitted myself to the people who could take me through it, but the burden of legalism had been removed, the idea that I had to achieve some mysterious state of Christian nirvana in order to obtain the blessing of God. Self-obsession died away and I became more able to receive.

I have grown tired of everything depending on me, and I reject any form of teaching that re-imposes that burden. This was never the Gospel. Freely you have received. Freely give. But too many of us stopped receiving and began laboring without the kind of receiving that would have energized our labor and enabled us to keep giving. We became Pharisees, and it made us self-centered because the only resources left were those we carried within ourselves.

How blessed are the people who know the joyful sound!
O LORD, they walk in the light of Your countenance.
In Your name they rejoice all the day.
And by Your righteousness they are exalted.
For You are the glory of their strength,
And by Your favor our horn is exalted.
For our shield belongs to the LORD,
And our king to the Holy One of Israel.

Psalm 89:15–18

Let Your work appear to Your servants
And Your majesty to their children.
Let the favor of the Lord our God be upon us;
And confirm for us the work of our hands;
Yes, confirm the work of our hands.

Psalm 90:16–17

It is time to lay it all down. The striving. The human effort. The legalism. Freely we have received. Now let us freely give. Let us recover the Gospel, received by grace in the wonderful river of the Father's love and then selflessly shared. It is all there in the cross and the blood! We need only plumb the depths of it.

9

Creating a Culture of Light

———————————•———————————

We are in the world, but not of the world, aren't we? And so we must leave behind the culture of self with all its demonic motivations and manifestations from lawlessness to legalism. But with what should we replace the self-focus we choose to repudiate? If we abandon the culture of the world and root it out of our fellowships, our families, our lives, our belief systems and practices, then what might the alternative look like?

"This is the message we have heard from Him and announce to you, that God is Light, and in Him there is no darkness at all" (1 John 1:5). From the beginning, from the moment God first called Abraham to Himself and began to form a people, He intended to create a culture of light that would be reflective of Himself and that would stand opposed to the culture of darkness dominant in the world. He envisioned this new nation as a different sort of people than the cultures surrounding them. They would live by a different pattern so that others would see and understand the truth about Himself as revealed in the nature of this chosen people of God. Yahweh would stand in sharp contrast to Baal, or Molech, or any other god because of the way this people lived and because of the visible favor He would lavish upon them.

This Old Testament destiny for the nation of Israel carries over into God's vision for the Church in the New Testament. Repeatedly in various ways Jesus says, "This is the way the world does things, but this is the way I want you to do things. Differently. Backward from the world's way." Where the world takes from one another, Jesus' people give. Where the world dominates and controls, the people of God serve. Where the world hates, the saints choose love.

The apostle Paul taught this different way of living in Philippians 2:14–16: "Do all things without grumbling or disputing; so that you will prove yourselves to be blameless and innocent, children of God above reproach in the midst of a crooked and perverse generation, among whom you appear as lights in the world, holding fast the word of life."

This world must come to know our Lord. In order for that to happen, we must become the attractive, winsome culture of light that we have not yet become.

The Role of Culture

Culture plays a major role in defining our understanding of who we are. One of the first things we come to know about ourselves as individuals, for example, is that we are white, Hispanic, African American, Native American, Asian and so on. Perhaps the most obvious thing we learn in connection with our racial origins is that race often defines who we are in differentiation from who others are, so that we make identity statements like, "I am black," or, "I am Latino." More often than not our racial identity, based in physical ancestry, brings with it a distinctive culture that defines us as individuals in ways of which we may be only vaguely aware. We develop a sense of individual belonging to a unique group of people who differentiate themselves from other groups of people on the basis of appearance and behavior. One's personal culture sets him or her apart from people of other cultures. We are not "them," and they are not "us."

Culture teaches us how to behave, compelling our behavior without any real awareness on our part that we are being compelled. Culture also programs the nature of relationships—husbands, wives, children and friends—as well as how we should feel and act with regard to various aspects and issues of life. We then act out what we have been taught, often without questioning our actions, because the pervasive force of our culture has built these things into us from the day we were born. These actions and behaviors seem right and proper to us, not because they are objectively right and proper, but because they are so much a part of us that they just feel self-evidently right and proper.

If you are from Texas, for example, you probably speak with an accent that clearly tells the rest of the world where you grew up. You never think about the way you speak. You do not intend to form your words with a drawl. Your culture taught you to speak that way, you absorbed it from those around you and so you do it rather naturally. In your personal perception of the world, everyone else has an accent, not you.

Many African Americans have been culturally conditioned by the long-term effects of slavery and prejudice. The black American heritage of oppression and suffering, for instance, has profoundly affected the way in which passion and emotion find expression in African American worship. Formed under oppression, partly as a much-needed emotional outlet, black culture plays a huge role in sustaining a unique style of free emotional expression in worship, passing it on from generation to generation, even to those who did not personally suffer in the same way that those who created the culture did. Each generation within the culture learns how to behave merely by being part of it. Culture touches every aspect of life. All of it just feels "right" because it was and is culture.

If you are Hispanic you may have been steeped in a culture that uniquely affects your value for interpersonal connections. While nearly everyone in a white neighborhood on a Saturday evening would be inside his home watching television in private or barbecuing in the backyard behind a seven-foot-high isolation fence, neighbors in a predominantly Hispanic area would more likely be outside on their front porches, talking with one another. The Hispanic culture itself holds a distinctive value for relationship.

If you are white and American, you have inherited a certain level of arrogance concerning your place in the world. You grew up with this as part of your cultural programming. It is woven into your attitudes, character and behavior at levels you probably have not even begun to realize. Being on top of the world just feels "right" to you, and it deeply and subconsciously conditions the way you relate to people of other races and cultures. You do not want to believe it does, but it does, and the strong probability is that you have never questioned it.

Culture conditions and programs behavior because it is the soup in which we live our daily lives. It is the pressure all around us—the words, hugs, attitudes, music, lifestyle,

commercials, billboards, newspaper headlines, outlays of
the stores in which we shop and types of clothing worn by
people around us. It all soaks in, permeating us at every
level until it becomes who and what we are by nature,
unquestioned. Culture teaches us ways to think, feel and
behave until these things feel right and normal to us because we grew up in them. Much of our behavior, both
good and bad, is therefore not genetic in origin, but rather
culturally conditioned.

Western Culture

No matter what racial or ethnic background we come
from, all of us in America—and perhaps the Western
world—share a common culture. Much of it is a culture
of self that affects us in the same way our ethnic cultures
do. It teaches us, for instance, that wealth and comfort
are a "must have" and that happiness cannot be obtained
without these things. It teaches us to focus on ourselves,
our personal feelings and our personal self-fulfillment.
We obey, instinctively and without question, serving Baal
without ever realizing it.

Worst of all, much of it is a culture of complaint, accusation and criticism flowing from our obsession with self.
Leadership by definition is suspect. We weigh and measure
one another and find one another wanting because we are
steeped in the demand that others serve our personal need
to be pleased and happy. Having thus passed judgment, we
then declare ourselves innocent or, at worst, victims.

At best, we see ourselves as justified in our judgments.
If I behaved badly, it was not my fault. I was a victim of
someone else's bad behavior, or I had a right to act that way
based on how I was treated or on the situation that confronted me. We have been marinated in a cultural soup of

complaint and grumbling in which nothing is ever enough
for us. It feels "right" to us to hold these attitudes because it
has been ingrained into us by our old nemesis, Baal, through
the pervasive cultural pressures that surround us.

Defining a Culture of Light

As believers in Jesus and heirs of the Abrahamic promise,
however, we have been called to a new culture—a culture
of sacrifice and giving, a culture of light. This new culture
would serve all the functions of culture in general to condition our sense of identity, behavior and attitudes, but the
result would be divinely and wonderfully different.

In order for it to become a culture, however, a significant
number of us who have been affected by the power and love
of God's Spirit must resign the culture of the world that is
steeped in self. We must become practitioners of the new
culture, permeated by the giving Spirit of Jesus and soaked
in His extreme mercy. Such a new culture must then grow
to become self-sustaining, fed by the Spirit of God and conditioning its members to godly character and attitude.

This culture would thrive on hunger for Jesus and the
experience of the Father's love, freely receiving and freely
giving. Where hunger for Him exists, the manifestation of
the presence of God follows. Where the manifestation of
the presence of God goes, the character of Jesus follows
and a culture emerges—a culture of light.

Scriptures for a New Cultural Identity

Ephesians 2 teaches us that in Jesus the races are now
one new man, a clear statement of cultural identity for the
new people of God:

For He Himself is our peace, who made both groups into one and broke down the barrier of the dividing wall . . . that in Himself He might make the two into one new man, thus establishing peace, and might reconcile them both in one body to God through the cross, by it having put to death the enmity.

verses 14–16

Peter also speaks of a new identity in Christ. Note the language of culture and "peoplehood":

You are a CHOSEN *RACE*, a royal *PRIESTHOOD*, A *HOLY NATION*, A *PEOPLE* FOR God's OWN POSSESSION, so that you may proclaim the excellencies of Him who has called you out of darkness into His marvelous light; for you once were NOT A *PEOPLE*, but now you are THE *PEOPLE* OF GOD; you had NOT RECEIVED MERCY, but now you have RECEIVED MERCY.

1 Peter 2:9–10, emphasis added

Chosen "race." Holy "nation." A "people." The foundation of the culture of the people Peter described (that which defines their identity and their behavior) is that they—we—are a people created for God's own possession. And we are a people with a purpose, to share the wonders we have experienced in Him.

Galatians 3 takes this a step further: "There is neither Jew nor Greek, there is neither slave nor free man, there is neither male nor female; for you are all one in Christ Jesus" (verse 28). There can be no black, white, Asian or Native American. There is only Christ Jesus. Redeemable elements of all our various earthly cultures then find their way into the expression of our faith and we rejoice in them as we should, but they no longer teach us who we are, nor do they any longer determine our behavior as a people.

150

Rather, they flow from our identification with our Lord and Savior.

New and Unique

In Him we have been called to create an entirely new and unique culture. The whole of the New Testament speaks of one. Aside from the call to make disciples, the great mission of the church—the one we have so often missed—is to create a new culture that serves all the functions of our old cultures in teaching us who we are and how to behave, feel and think.

It must be informed by the Spirit of God and be just as pervasively compelling as our old cultures have been to form and shape those who become a part of it. It must stand against the culture of the world, which has been steeped in complaint, accusation, grumbling, self and pride. It must be a culture founded in blessing, flowing from the living and loving presence of the Holy Spirit. As fathers in Bible times determined the nature of their families, so we must derive our nature from the overwhelming river of the Father's love. For that reason alone, we desperately need revival, do we not?

My son, Nathan, serves as youth pastor on our church staff. Three years ago he had an impossible group of kids. They were out of control and uninterested in the things of God. They brought drugs to their meetings. Many physically and verbally abused one another. Some of them sexually violated one another in the restrooms. One night the group flooded en masse out of the youth room to run up the street for a gang fight. Many times I saw Nathan collapse in tears of despair. Over and over again I exhorted him not to quit.

It boiled down to a conflict of cultures. Outside the church, the lost and demonically energized youth culture kept claiming the lives we were trying to save. I counseled Nathan that we needed to create a culture of our own and then steep the kids in it, replacing godless influence from the culture of darkness with godly conditioning from a culture of light. Some might call it positive peer pressure, but it is more than that.

The first part of the solution was to stop focusing on the obvious leaders, the popular kids who refused to turn to Jesus, and to begin focusing on those who demonstrated a hunger for God in their visible worship by the questions they asked and by their faithfulness. They turned out to be mostly the outcasts, the nerds, the unlikely and outwardly ungifted. Sounds like something Jesus might do, doesn't it? The old crowd mostly left when they found they could no longer be the center of attention or control what God was doing.

As a culture of radical love and acceptance took root, the group exploded. The Spirit of God broke out and we saw four hundred percent growth in less than a year. Kids who had never considered God heard voices calling them to go to the church. They came, got saved, got blasted by the Spirit of God and began speaking in tongues before they had even heard of that gift. A culture of light developed that taught love, respect, godliness and morality.

Today we have youth on our altar ministry teams and our prophetic ministry teams. On their own initiative, our youth take care packages to the poor and homeless in the inner city. They set the pace for the congregation in worship. God graced us to create a culture of light to combat the culture of darkness, and it works. The Body of Christ at large needs the same kind of transformation.

What the Culture of Light Looks Like

When the Holy Spirit comes, He reveals Jesus. John 16:14 teaches, "He will glorify Me, for He will take of Mine and will disclose it to you." The center of this culture must therefore be the Person of Jesus in whom the Father's love is perfectly revealed. Nothing else really matters. His Presence defines it. His Spirit gives it life and causes it to function. Without the Spirit of Jesus, such a culture will ever remain an impossibility, a distant dream never realized.

The Spirit eternally praises the Father and the Son, which makes this culture a culture of praise. We must study the works of God, sing of them and speak of them wherever we go. In doing so we will effectively defeat the spirit of complaint and criticism that so often captivates us. When the good moves in, the bad moves out.

In studying the works of God, we open our eyes to the whole picture—all that God is doing—rather than practicing a fixation on what we perceive to be lacking. This culture of light must live in the things that God is clearly accomplishing, not in what we do not yet see Him doing. Praise and worship play a major role in keeping that focus alive. Those who desire to be in the presence of the Holy Spirit must learn to live in a perpetual state of worship. The culture of light will be a culture of praise.

The Holy Spirit is always building people. Is not edification what the gifts of the Holy Spirit are all about? When He reveals Himself, when He begins to move, when we feel His Presence, aren't people built up, restored and healed? Isn't it interesting that almost every place in Scripture that speaks of the gifts of the Holy Spirit also speaks of strengthening or equipping people, building up the fellowship of the saints, encouraging, exhorting and lifting? People in a culture of light edify one another as they leave behind the culture that teaches them to edify themselves.

Our Lord longs to build a truly Christian—not religious—culture, a culture of light, a culture of praise and a culture of grace in which the pervasive atmosphere of His presence molds individuals into a connected people fixed on Jesus and steeped in His love. These principles are illustrated beautifully in Romans 12, 1 Corinthians 12–13 and Philippians 2.

It all points to a culture that cradles us in servanthood, encourages, heals, praises and lifts up, a culture focused on the worship of Jesus, praising the works of God and strengthening His disciples. If each of us lived immersed in such a culture, would we not become blessedly infected with it, until the dictates of that culture came to feel instinctively right and natural to us?

Second-Nature Goodness

Remember that the culture in which we live conditions our thoughts, actions and ways of doing things until that conditioning becomes second nature to us. I have already described how we speak with an accent because we have learned our patterns of speech from the culture that surrounds us. How wonderful it would be if the culture surrounding us in the Body of Christ were so infused with the character of Jesus that everything we did carried His "accent"! The Jesus accent would be an accent of love and freedom.

In a culture of light, when a brother fails or stumbles, we forgive him, love him and encourage him instead of criticizing him and talking to others about his failure. In a culture of light we do this instinctively because it feels right to do it as we are infused with the Spirit of Jesus who carries His character. It feels right to do it because our culture, our culture of light, permeated with His presence, teaches and conditions us to do it. It teaches us selflessness.

In the same way that we can be caught up in a culture of the world, we can be caught up in a culture of light and so become a people of blessing. It ought to become second nature to us. We will still be sinners in need of constant vigilance, grace and repentance, but if strife and criticism can become a cultural contagion, why can't exhortation, love and encouragement? Aren't we carried along, strengthened and taught by the atmosphere in which we live?

A Culture of Favor

When the Church of Jesus Christ becomes a people of blessing in a culture of blessing, a nation within a nation, and when that nation is all about the nature of Jesus, then all God's people draw favor from the world around them because blessing given is favor received. We see this clearly demonstrated in the life of the early Church:

> They were continually devoting themselves to the apostles' teaching and to fellowship, to the breaking of bread and to prayer. Everyone kept feeling a sense of awe; and many wonders and signs were taking place through the apostles. And all those who had believed were together and had all things in common; and they began selling their property and possessions and were sharing them with all, as anyone might have need. Day by day continuing with one mind in the temple, and breaking bread from house to house, they were taking their meals together with gladness and sincerity of heart, praising God and having favor with all the people. And the Lord was adding to their number day by day those who were being saved.
>
> Acts 2:42–47

In the Old Testament, five hundred years before Christ, Daniel became the key advisor to the foreign king, who was leader of the conquerors of Daniel's nation and a man worthy of hatred. Daniel obtained favor and position with this king because he chose to selflessly serve him in the Lord through his God-given gift of interpreting dreams (see Daniel 2). Daniel understood that in the Lord's economy, blessing given is favor received, even—or especially—when the one to whom we give the blessing is undeserving.

"Give, and it will be given to you. They will pour into your lap a good measure—pressed down, shaken together, and running over" (Luke 6:38). Blessing given is favor received.

Let's Do It!

We must cultivate a culture of giving, in which a pervasive atmosphere of sacrifice immerses every member in a lifestyle of sacrificial giving until selflessness comes as naturally to the individual participant as the accent with which we speak. Self-sacrifice in love must flow as effortlessly for us as the way a member of an African culture might learn to dance with freedom or as easily as the way a member of a Hispanic culture might learn to enjoy salsa music.

We will do these culturally conditioned things because we feel "right" doing them. They seep into our very bones because in a culture of light they are all around us. What if giving, blessing, praising and loving the presence of the Lord were to surround us in the same pervasive way as the influences of the secular cultures in which we live? What if these "Jesus things" actually became the culture of this "nation" we call the Church, pervasively influencing us every day and conditioning us to the character of

Jesus? The culture of self would be defeated, and what God intended from the day He first called Abraham would victoriously emerge.

If this became reality, then new believers entering into this culture of light would absorb its influences from and through us with no conscious awareness of what they were absorbing. They would simply catch it from other members of the culture until it became an integral part of their character. It would seem natural and normal to behave, to feel, to think in the new ways taught, modeled and reinforced by others. It would be "the thing to do," wouldn't it? As this culture took root in all of us, the world would look on in wonder and grant favor to God's people, as it did the Church in Acts 2. It would be a marvelously compelling form of evangelism.

A people of blessing! A culture of faith! A nation whose identity derives entirely from the life and Spirit of the Lord Jesus Christ! Let's do it. Let's be it. It is what God is looking for.

10

The Next Move of God in Worship

———————————•———————————

Why would I include a chapter on worship in a book prophetically addressing the self-focus of a church culture infected by the values of the world? Because worship has been conditioned by that same culture. Because worship forms the connection between us and God that energizes everything else we do.

But that which should be a selfless sacrifice offered to God for God's sake has too often become a slick platform event directed more at entertaining and attracting people than at pleasing and blessing the living God. We have become audiences who observe rather than congregations who participate. It is too often about what we *get* from worship than about what we *give* to God as an act of loving sacrifice, more about what we take from the event than an experience we share with the Lord. That would be Baal's way, wouldn't it?

In too much of the Christian world, "psalm" has become merely "song." What ought to be "spiritual song" has become just "music." What Jesus intended to be an intimate meeting between Himself and His beloved bride has become a "worship set," a term borrowed from the world of the professional musician to describe the group of songs he performs before taking a break or ending the concert. It speaks of performance, rather than the intimate relationship God has in mind.

In late 2004, I received a scathing prophetic word via email from my father, with whom I have shared a common view of the Church for many years. Here are some excerpts:

> Many Christians in [renewal movements] are seeking selfishly [in worship], experiencing thrills which keep them seeking thrills, but most of it is soulish and self-centered . . . I think there is a stronghold of self-centered selfishness at the core . . . "God is going to do for us and that is why we are here, but do not expect us to live self-sacrificially day by day in disciplined lives of service to others." A few get that, but most just want the goose bumps and the great feelings, not the cost. I have been watching worshipers in major cities across the country, and what I see is people excitedly rejoicing and dancing in God's presence, enjoying the worship—but when I ask myself, "How much of this is really to bless God, for His sake? How much of this really pleases Him? How much is really for Him to bless His heart?" The answer I get is, "Very little." . . . We thrill ourselves with experiences and call that worship. Something is wrong at the core. It is promoting selfishness rather than daily sacrifice for Him; [it is] not worship that is really tuned in to bless Him for His sake. There has just been too much of, "get, get, get," and, "experience, experience, experience,"

rather than, "Be there to bless Him and others, whatever the cost, whether you feel anything or not."

Baal religion offers sacrifices in order to get something for self. Worship that is focused on self, rather than God, can never be more than Baal religion. It can be only a transaction, never a real relationship.

But worship of God in Spirit and in truth seeks to please the God we love. This kind of worship is pure intimacy. How I long for the worship of heaven! How I long for the day when we truly meet and bless our awesome God just for the sake of seeing His pleasure!

Catering to the Culture

At the other end of the stylistic divide, in "seeker sensitive" circles the philosophy states that because the unbeliever and the outsider cannot relate to extended worship, we must cut it short. We must hold it down to maybe three songs, so that we can attract and keep those coming from the secular culture. In this we not only believe we must cater to the culture of self, but we also believe we are actually doing it. Wrong on both counts!

Two years ago, I paid a lot of money to see my favorite singer/songwriter perform at the Chatauqua auditorium in Boulder, Colorado. This artist is a closet Christian and some of his songs carry spiritual or even openly Christian themes. The place was packed with fifteen hundred New Agers who had paid the same exorbitant amount of money as I had to sit and listen to one man for two hours.

Alone on that stage, he held that audience of the unbelieving spellbound with nothing more than his guitar, his voice and his engaging wit. No light show, no choreo-

160

graphed dancers, no backup band. At the end they called him out for three curtain calls.

Switch on MTV during a televised concert and you will see thousands of young people pulsating to the music with their hands in the air for two hours. It looks disturbingly like powerful and enthusiastic worship!

I see these things in the world and conclude that we must not allow ourselves to believe that the outsider and the unbeliever cannot relate to extended times of worship. They can. The truth is that they cannot endure our failure to inspire. They reject our lack of excellence in presentation. They do not relate to our isolated musical genre that speaks no language they can understand. They will come and stay for an experience of God, if that experience is available—and we pray they move beyond it and into a love of God for God's sake. They will come for a quality presentation and a tangible sense of the presence of God, and they will remain transfixed by it for hours at a time, but we are going to have to make some changes to provide the kind of worship experience worthy of their time.

We live in a culture increasingly hungry for the supernatural experience of the living God, but we in the Church are mostly failing to provide it in a package "average Joe" can recognize. In too many cases we are failing to provide it at all.

Truncated worship and watered-down messages just will not do. We must rediscover the experience, value and glory of worship that speaks into the culture around us while remaining steeped in the wonder of the culture of light and given to the Lord for the Lord's own sake. It can and should be culture-current in style, but it must never be culturally determined in spirit, either by the culture of the world or by the culture of religion.

New Things Coming

As I have studied the book of Revelation, one of the things I have noticed is how frequently heavenly worship in all its extreme intensity manifests in John's accounts of the unfolding end times. John saw glorious heavenly scenes of martyrs—those who gave the last full selfless measure of devotion—with harps and golden bowls, together with millions upon millions of angels and earthly creatures worshipping with a deafening roar. In his vision the glory of God filled the heavenly temple until no one could stand to be in the center of it.

Are we living in the last days as John foresaw them? Will we see a new movement of intensified and heavenly worship in the days leading up to the return of the Lord? I hope so. A new tsunami wave of the Spirit of God is building, but it will not be more of the same or a repeat of the past. In days to come there will be a significant shift in the flow of the river of God's Spirit. At the heart of this shift will be a new depth in worship. A new quality and a new anointing will soon emerge, freed from the shackles and chains of the wrong-headed and misguided philosophies and theologies of the past.

In the worship of my own church since 1997, we have experienced audible angel song and heard angelic flutes where none existed in the natural. Since mid-2002 we even have seen feathers falling through the air. In spring 2004, the glory fell during worship and sovereign healings resulted without benefit of prayer or laying on of hands. These days it seems God's favorite time to do ministry to hearts and bodies in need is right in the midst of the flow of worship. The team keeps playing and the congregation worships. The front of the auditorium fills with those responding to the call and our ministry team goes to work.

162

And why not? Jesus loves us and we love Him back. Then He loves us some more. It is not unusual these days to sing, rather than speak, words of knowledge or healing over those who come forward. One night the Lord gave me a spontaneous song complete with rhyming verses as a word of knowledge for some who had been away and were coming back. The theme was "Welcome Home." By the end of it, several had come forward in tears to receive ministry on that issue. By the time worship ends, the floor at the front of the auditorium is often carpeted with bodies lying deep in the presence of the Lord.

This sort of worship requires a fresh approach. Those who lead it must walk in the sort of intimacy with God that enables them to "hear" the music of heaven with their heart and spirit, and they must have both the freedom and the musical skills to spontaneously recreate what they hear in the moment. This requires a level of gifting, intimacy and anointing that empowers them to simultaneously hear from heaven, sense the people and create the music for the Lord's sake to draw in the congregation.

In this intimacy, that which we have come to call "song of the Lord" becomes a glorious, spontaneous, creative outpouring. In my own congregation some of our best-established worship songs have first emerged as "songs of the Lord," complete with melodic "hook" and rhyming lyrics. I know of other congregations experiencing the same sort of thing and growing in it, but it is not yet as common as it is going to become.

None of this is as difficult as it might sound, although it does require a high level of musicianship and a musical box full of "tools" to call upon—loose riffs, melodies and good musical sense, stored up in the heart—but it is more important that we seek the intimacy with God and the godly character necessary to pull it off. Heaven sings to us, but we must learn how to listen.

The culture of self and the influence of Baal ambush and sabotage many musicians who try to lead worship in the way I describe. Baal makes the experience all about the musician's personal creativity, expression and feelings. Musicians can be the most self-centered, dysfunctional, troubled and emotive people on the planet. With these influences at work, the platform can very quickly become a venue for self-validation rather than sacrifice. Musicians in worship must set their hearts to lead others into the presence of the Lord, rather than to merely self-express. They must mediate the Presence as priests of the Lord rather than perform. There is a choice to be made. Will we be priestly worshippers or just musicians?

Hebrews, God and Worship

The culture in which we live communicates a concept of God that ultimately affects the way we express ourselves in worship. Worship style, as differentiated from genre, inevitably reflects our concept of God. Simply put, our expression of worship looks very much like our vision of the nature of the Almighty.

But our concept of God is determined by two primary cultural factors. On the one hand we live every day in a culture steeped in a focus on self, while on the other we have inherited a concept of God conditioned by seventeen or eighteen centuries of history, which also has become part of our culture, whether we are aware of it or not. To better understand these historical influences, we must take a brief tour of history.

It did not take long, less than the lifetime of the original apostles, for the Gospel to spread beyond the confines of

Judaism in Palestine to become predominantly a religion of the *goyyim*—the Gentiles or non-Jews, "the nations." This means that Christian faith moved into a world holding different fundamental understandings of reality and spirituality than those of the Jewish milieu from which it sprang, or of the Hebrew Bible that undergirded it.

A Heart of Passion

Scripture, written by Hebrews about Hebrews from a Hebrew cultural perspective, presents God as passionate and emotional, involved in the affairs of men and bound to them in a love covenant. God comes to Moses in Exodus 3 in the midst of the burning bush to call him to go down to Egypt and lead the people out of slavery. He introduces Himself as "I AM"—the One who is present, rather than distant and removed. In verse 16, He says to Moses, "I am indeed concerned about you and what has been done to you in Egypt." This is a God who cares and loves passionately and who feels compelled to act on that care and love.

In Exodus 4:14, God has had enough of Moses' arguing with Him. Scripture says, "The anger of the LORD burned against Moses." Here is a God of passion, His very essence emotional, and He expresses those emotions quite openly. On hundreds of occasions the Bible speaks of the Lord's compassion. Two or three hundred references speak to His lovingkindness, and there are as many references to His mercy. All of these spring from a heart of passion and strong feeling.

"For God so loved the world" (John 3:16). Again we see the strength of feeling that drives the passionate God to act and to involve Himself in the affairs of this earth. Is this quality of "love" in the heart of God merely some sort of rational, reasoned, restrained, intellectual construct without real emotional content? Or is it more like what I feel while holding my newest grandchild tenderly in my arms, gazing into her soft newborn face and then into the face of her father until the tears begin to roll? Isn't it Father God at Jesus' baptism crying out in love-filled pleasure, "This is My beloved Son, in whom I am well-pleased" (Matthew 3:17)? Wasn't it an act of extreme passion that He so deeply loved the world that He gave this same only Son to die in our place?

The Bible paints many pictures of the nature of worship in ancient Israel. In them we see a passion for God in worship repeatedly demonstrated in outward, physically expressive acts reflective of the Hebrew concept of God Himself as passionate and emotive.

Hebrews and Spontaneous Passionate Worship

After Israel had escaped Pharaoh by crossing the Red Sea with the water standing like walls on either side, Exodus 15:20 says, "Miriam the prophetess, Aaron's sister, took the timbrel in her hand, and all the women went out after her with timbrels and with dancing." Filled to overflowing with joy, they danced while she sang a long and beautiful song to the Lord, seemingly composed spontaneously, as an outpouring of overwhelming gratitude. Scriptural worship abounds with emotional demonstration expressed physically, the joy of deliverance loosed and acted out, often unrehearsed and fresh in its expression.

In 2 Samuel 6, David brought the Ark of the Lord into his capital city of Jerusalem. As he led the procession, Scripture says in verses 14–15,

David was dancing before the LORD with all his might, and David was wearing a linen ephod. So David and all the

166

house of Israel were bringing up the ark of the LORD with shouting and the sound of the trumpet.

Here we see passionate, loud and unrestrained physical demonstrations of emotion.

Second Chronicles gives us more pictures of the unrestrained worship of the Hebrew people:

All the Levitical singers . . . and their sons and kinsmen, clothed in fine linen, with cymbals, harps and lyres, standing east of the altar, and with them one hundred and twenty priests blowing trumpets in unison when the trumpeters and the singers were to make themselves heard with one voice to praise and to glorify the LORD, and when they lifted up their voice accompanied by trumpets and cymbals and instruments of music, and when they praised the LORD saying, "He indeed is good for His lovingkindness is everlasting," then the house, the house of the LORD, was filled with a cloud, so that the priests could not stand to minister because of the cloud, for the glory of the LORD filled the house of God.

2 Chronicles 5:12–14

Now when Solomon had finished praying, fire came down from heaven and consumed the burnt offering and the sacrifices, and the glory of the LORD filled the house. The priests could not enter into the house of the LORD because the glory of the LORD filled the LORD's house. All the sons of Israel, seeing the fire come down and the glory of the LORD upon the house, bowed down on the pavement with their faces to the ground, and they worshiped and gave praise to the LORD, saying, "Truly He is good, truly His lovingkindness is everlasting."

2 Chronicles 7:1–3

When have any of us seen such wonders on a Sunday morning? The Scriptures abound with dancing, shouting and singing—loudly!—as well as extravagant sacrifices of animals and goods, all of it passion filled. It includes weeping, priests falling down before the Lord—not getting down but falling down—shouting and even the sense of smell as incense burned on the altar.

The Hebrews conceived of God as present, passionate and emotional in every way, and their worship reflected that understanding. They made their worship physically demonstrative and loudly vocal because the human voice, and the expression of it in singing, connects the heart and draws out the emotions. Dancing likewise connects the body outwardly to our inward emotions in order to express and expose them.

Historic Cultural Conditioning in the Western World

As Christianity, which began among Jewish people for whom emotional demonstration and expression of passion were items of faith, passed into the Gentile world, it began to absorb elements of a foreign philosophy. Some of that philosophy held that the physical body is evil in and of itself and therefore must be subdued and denied. Physical expression of emotion therefore became a negative thing, as did sex and sexual feelings. According to the dominant philosophy of the Greek world, these were to be suppressed and avoided.

As the Roman Empire fell into decay and the order it had established began to fall apart, the Dark Ages descended upon Europe and continued for eight hundred years, from approximately 500 AD into the first half of the second millennium. Chaos reigned. People suffered. Plague wiped out millions of people in a time of darkness and fear that had never been seen in the Western world—nor has since. Life seemed not joyous, but grievous. Physical existence seemed confirmed as an evil thing, a prison of weakness and suffering from which to seek escape.

Early in this period, the Church built upon the idea that the body is bad and that passion is evil. Understandably it began to believe in a distant God without passion, undisturbed by any suffering or emotion. Orderly and controlled, His peace meant that He did not feel. This God remained eternally transcendent, above all these things that so troubled human beings.

The Impact on Worship

Expressions of worship inevitably came to reflect this developing philosophy of a distant and dispassionate God. Gregorian chant, for example, circa 600 AD, was designed intentionally as a subdued and passionless form of worship reflective of the cultural concept of a God untouched by human passions and pain. This form of worship sought to create a sense of peace, holding no real emotion in its transcendence of the physical world. Liturgies were developed in order to appropriately approach a dispassionate God of order in an orderly way. Spontaneous outbursts of emotion in worship were considered irreverent and became illegal. The truly holy would never be troubled by all that mess.

Western Christian worship has never fully recovered from that mind-set, nor has our culture in general. For more than a millennium and a half, one of the fundamental tenets of Western culture has been repression of passion and emotion. I say repression, not elimination. While we have become a culture of self, fixated on our individual emotional states, we continue to live with a cultural bias against unrestrained emotional demonstration, which has led to erroneous interpretations of Paul's comments in 1 Corinthians 14, for instance, concerning order in the assembly. This same cultural bias forms the basis for much of the criticism leveled at past and present revival manifestations, so carefully couched in proper-sounding theological terms. To our culturally conditioned eyes, these things are just too messy to be regarded as legitimately divine.

Under the pressure of this conditioning, it has therefore become a principle of holiness, a self-evident truth among the peoples of Western nations, that we must behave ourselves in the house of God. Infected by the history of Western theology and our concept of God, our culture erroneously defines reverence as quiet dignity. Nothing must be allowed to happen in the house of God that seems out of control, because our hearts know that we simply do not behave that way in the presence of the dignified, distant and dispassionate God. We sit at strict attention and fix our gazes straight ahead. We kneel when told and recite the liturgy when given permission to speak. If the pastor sees one of us weeping while all this is going on, he seeks that one out following the service, certain that something must be wrong for such an emotional display to have burst the bonds of holy reserve.

Under the pressure of all this history and culture, if you feel—and especially if you feel deeply—then you have learned to keep it to yourself. You contain it. At best, you let it out only in safely measured quantities. Why? Because you have learned that the nature of God is somehow distant and dispassionate, that He really does not feel passionately. He is somehow removed from all that messy confusion we call feelings.

Where We Learned It

We learned this concept of God not from Scripture but from our culture. As children we were taught to suck it up when feelings overwhelmed our fledgling control mechanisms. If we laughed and played too loudly with too much exuberance or reckless abandon, our parents told us to be quiet and go to our rooms. If we were too prone to tears, they told us, "Stop that crying or I'll give you something to cry about." If we ran through the aisles and between the pews in the sanctuary as children, we were sternly rebuked. That was just not an appropriate way to behave in church! "What is the matter with you? This is God's house!"

But what is so wrong with running in the house of God? Why not express exuberance in His presence? David, king of Israel, did it—or something like it! Children sense the presence of the Lord instinctively, more easily than we controlled adults do. In the Lord's sanctuary they often respond to that presence with an unfettered emotional up-rush, which they express physically until we crush it out of them by teaching them that God does not like spontaneous outbursts of emotion. Bottle it up! Keep it capped!

Men do not cry. And women are inferior because they are more emotional than men. Isn't that what our culture still tells us? By our cultural definition, feelings are at best unreliable and at worst silly. Even after decades of effort to free ourselves, these attitudes remain embedded in us, robbing us of our freedom.

What We Really Believe about God

Because our culture has had these attitudes for 1500 years, we remain mired in the belief that God is not just cold, dispassionate and unfeeling, but also harsh and judgmental, certainly not compassionate and definitely not warm. We have always said that He is loving, and we do not want to admit that we really believe what we really believe, but too little in our practice and expression of worship has actually reflected warmth and compassion. In 1992, the executive pastor of a very large church known for its contemporary style was ordered by his senior pastor to go stop the lone woman dancing with lovely abandon before the altar during a time of deep worship. She was "distracting." I rest my case. We all should have joined her!

If what we believe about the nature of God determines our expression of worship, then conversely our expression of worship reveals what we really believe about God. Because we cannot fully connect with the fullness of God in His emotional nature, our only alternative is to sink into the religious spirit in which we judge sinners without mercy. Because we really believe God to be dispassionate, we mercilessly pass judgment even on one another. Often when every other emotion has become illegal to freely express, only anger remains, which we then visit on other members of the Body of Christ.

Our concept of God expressed in worship teaches us to line up in neat straight rows, to sing when told, to hold the hymnal carefully, never looking up, to clothe ourselves in suits, ties and dresses for worship because we believe that pleases God. Formal and organized, it all reflects passionless order. This is how we have believed God Himself to be.

In recent decades, we have grown past the suits, ties and hymnals but not the restraint. Not really. In reality we have simply adopted another version of informal formality in the presence of God. We all know exactly what to do and what not to do every time we gather, and when revival manifestations disrupt that order we tend to cry out in criticism that God would never inspire such things. He is, after all, a God of order.

The Nature of Restraint

Earning a bachelor's degree in vocal music gave me a sense of the sweep of musical history. Until the last century, the history of music was largely the history of the Church, so it is not difficult to track. As I have already pointed out, Gregorian chant from the Middle Ages was transcendently passionless. Renaissance music for the Church (beginning in the fifteenth century) reflected God's glory, but not His passion. In college we were taught that in order to sing a Renaissance mass properly, we must feel the passion, but bottle it up and restrain the feeling. The baroque period that followed in the seventeenth and eighteenth centuries—Bach and Beethoven—developed forms and rules for expression. It held more passion but remained restrained. After that came the classical period with a form so perfect it seemed nearly sterile. Passion was clearly present but frozen and restrained in a closely governed form. The structures of Western worship have never allowed a real Davidic expression of freedom. Even in the contemporary renewal we remain contained.

Some of us refuse to sing, and consequently we do not really worship. It feels insurmountably strange to some of us to let go and allow our voices to soar. Maybe you think it is because you do not sing well, but I do not believe that is the real reason. The truth is that most of us who do not sing just do not know how to let our hearts feel freely, much less express that feeling in a physical way. As I said earlier, if you really opened your mouth and let your voice soar with power, it would connect you emotionally, drawing out feelings for you to experience and for all to see. At the deepest levels of your soul, you are much too self-absorbed and self-conscious to allow that to happen. This was built into you by means of the dual pressure of the culture of self on the one hand and the culture of religion on the other. Such restraint therefore seems "right" to you, while freedom seems awkward, embarrassing and even ungodly.

If you were to get out of your chair and dance, the same thing would happen. Bodily expression would connect with your hidden feelings and draw them out. To a lesser degree, lifting your hands can have the same effect, except that lifting hands in worship has now become universally acceptable in the Body of Christ—part of the ritual, like kneeling at a Catholic mass. Physical actions release emotions, but we have been taught to be afraid of the release.

As a result, to keep from feeling anything you might not be able to contain, you just do not participate demonstrably or visibly in corporate worship. You become a spectator, holding the whole experience at a safe and controlled distance. Worship in too much of the contemporary Church has consequently degenerated into neatly packaged Christian entertainment in which the Body of Christ becomes a mass of spectators—moved but not really participating. Someone "up there" is doing it for us. "Self" is served and entertained while control is properly maintained.

Where the culture of self plays into this takes us back to the beginning of the chapter. It all becomes not a sacrifice to God offered for His sake but a contained cultural event aimed at serving the needs of the worshippers. I have stated that our forms of worship ultimately reflect our concept of God, so now we have added to our concept of God the idea that God is there to serve us, to obey the needs of self. Rather than an act of sacrifice, worship therefore becomes something the believer must get something out of for his or her own sake.

We therefore become imprisoned in our worship from two sides—the concept that God is a distant and removed God of order on the one hand, and the heavenly sugar daddy existing to serve our personal needs and agendas on the other hand. Caught in this cultural squeeze play, we miss the true wonder and glory.

Please do not read judgment or condemnation into any of this. I merely point out what our culture has taught us. I long for my own freedom. Like most of you, I have lost something, and I want it back. We have been too crippled in our ability to allow holy and wholesome emotions to live, much less find physical and visible expression, and we have been trapped by all we have learned in the culture of self.

The bulk of this deficit has its root in faulty or incomplete concepts of God that have been passed on for centuries. Unfortunately our cultural perception of the nature of God really has not changed much historically, and in those elements where it has changed, the additions have often not been helpful.

Exceptions to Restraint

In some corners of Western culture we see less restraint, but not much. The Methodist church I served as a youth pastor fresh out of seminary was overwhelmingly white, but the choir director was an African American woman. In addition to her post as music director at Hope United Methodist Church, she led an all-black choir called Voices of Faith. Each year in December, she brought the white Methodist choir together with the black Voices of Faith for a magnificent Christmas concert.

Across the back row stood the black choir, swaying with the music, clapping and exclaiming loudly, "Sing it, sister!" during passionate solos. In front of them stood a row or two of older, very "together" and very white Methodist women, hands folded, looking for all the world like a truck was about to run them over from behind, loving it, but functionally unable to loosen up and let it happen to them. Black culture in America makes some room for free emotional expression, at least in music, but I suspect not much more at many other levels. We have lived together on this continent too long not to be affected by the anti-experiential, anti-emotional bias of the dominant culture.

In the midst of this, I thought I was pretty "with it," until the director asked me to sing "Silent Night" *a capella*. I sang it "white," and she never let me sing it again. I have learned some freedom since then, but I am not yet where I want to be.

What We Really Fear

When we shy away from rowdy, noisy worship and the manifestations that sometimes come with it, we are not really avoiding the expressions themselves but rather what they represent. Unrestrained or passionate demonstrations of emotion threaten us. It all started with the idea that God Himself was like that. Restrained. Distant. Without feeling. Above all that messy stuff we call emotion.

The real reason so many Christians object to outpourings of the Spirit of God, such as those we have seen in Toronto and Pensacola, has nothing to do with manifestations of the Spirit and all the arguments we have heard and read that question the biblical basis of falling, shaking and laughing. The real objection is that our culture has subtly, deeply and effectively taught us to believe in a non-emotional God, unmoved by all that moves us, and that we must therefore be restrained as well. We have absorbed this training so deeply that it now feels self-evident to us that anything not restrained, anything not perfectly ordered and unemotional, cannot be of God. Open physical expressions of passion and emotion that follow upon revival represent things not so controlled. The dominant culture therefore opposes them.

With this bias so deeply seated within us, the Church has a tendency to read into the Scriptures forms of restraint, order and lack of passion that are not really there. We are blind to the truth because the pervasive and subtle pressure of the culture has made the counterfeit seem so right.

Many of us like it quiet and meditative because we can live with and control quiet and meditative feelings. Clearly Scripture makes room for the quiet and the meditative. We need the seasons of intimacy we find in quietness, but Scripture also shows us explosions of worshipful passion into outrageous physical demonstrations. With such explosions comes power—and glory with it.

I believe that the double whammy of our cultural concept of God as passionless and distant, together with our cultural fixation on self, has been diabolically designed to limit the glory, the full revelation of who God is. We cannot fully worship the Lord if we cannot allow feelings to flow freely in open expression. Fear holds us back.

But we will need the glory in the days to come. God longs to send it. I pray every Sunday that God will come and wreck our meetings, take them beyond our control. It is His house, not ours. I desperately want Him to be Him, to see Him and experience Him as He is and not through the filter of a culture, whether old or new.

In Spirit and in Truth

Wouldn't it be reasonable to assume that this demonstrated passion has something to do with what Jesus meant when He spoke to the woman at the well in Samaria?

"An hour is coming, and now is, when the true worshipers will worship the Father in spirit and truth; for such people the Father seeks to be His worshipers. God is spirit, and those who worship Him must worship in spirit and truth."

John 4:23–24

Because God is Spirit, we must worship Him in spirit. In other words, worship must reflect the fullness of the nature of God. All that He is in His Spirit must find expression in our worship. Worship in spirit and in truth cannot therefore be viewed as merely holding a proper set of beliefs. Against the backdrop of the sweep of Scripture, Jesus spoke of a depth of worship that connects us with the nature of God in all that He is at the core of all that we are.

When We Perceive Him as He Is

When worship is whole, when it is reflective of who God really is, when it is unrestrained as an offering of the full heart, mind and soul and when it is offered for His sake as a sacrifice to Him, then physical manifestations of His presence often follow. One of the components of the turning of our youth group was a breakthrough in worship. In autumn 2002, after months of prayer, the Spirit of God struck like a sudden hurricane, sweeping the group into two hours of powerful worship on the first night of the outpouring. So loud was their singing and shouting to the Lord that the neighbors across the street called the police.

Our Sunday night renewal services have seen the manifestations of which I have already spoken. I am beginning to hear similar stories from other churches. I know of one Texas congregation that will never paint the walls of its sanctuary again because of the gold dust that has appeared on them. Worship in spirit and in truth can produce physical demonstrations of His presence.

The Coming Shift in Worship

The coming shift in anointing on the Body of Christ, the next outpouring of His Spirit, will be for those who worship in spirit and in truth as an act of sacrifice for God's own sake in selfless abandon, who understand God as a real and passionate Person, who grant themselves the freedom to meet the sacrificial passion of God with sacrificial passion from their own hearts. It will be for those who free themselves from the gospel of self and who therefore give to God for God's own sake. This new outpouring of God's Spirit will take us to new places in our experience and in the manifestation of His presence. It will be rooted in worship and flow from worship into all the gifts and ministries of the Church.

No longer will it be possible to focus only on prophetic gifts and prophetic issues while simply observing the worship of others. Prophetic ministry will flow from worship, from the intimacy and freedom of passion-filled communion with Jesus. Likewise, healing ministry will cease to be a stand-alone anointing in the context of the Church. Increasingly it will flow from the power of worship and will manifest in that context, during worship and under the power of the Spirit in worship. Worship—extended, powerful, passion-filled, lingering worship offered to God not as entertainment, but for God's own sake in sacrifice—will bring the glory, and in the glory we will see miracles happen.

The same will be true of every other ministry of the Church. Worship will be the fountainhead. No longer just the warm-up for the sermon, it will stand as the main course on an equal footing with the preaching of the Word. Power will result so that worship will become a major force in overcoming the self-focus of the dominant culture around us.

So let's be truly biblical in our worship and in our concept of the Father God. Let's go deeper. Let's seek expressions of worship to reflect the reality of all the passion that is God's and the selfless sacrifice that is His nature. Let's seek freedom of emotion together with freedom to express it. Let's not permit our worship to be limited by what our culture has taught us, but let us rather walk in that which God Himself has revealed concerning Himself. If we do this, I believe we can expect to see more visible evidence of His presence.

11

Choosing Revival

The culture of self wants God to come, but only on its own terms and in ways palatable to its sense of comfort and control. It says, "God, come for me," rather than, "Lord, build Your Kingdom." God desperately longs to pour out revival upon us—but only on His own terms, in His own way and for His own purposes. Historically this has always been an offense to the prevailing religious culture, and so it is now.

Recent Revival in North America

In January 1994, in response to the prayers of thousands of faithful saints and intercessors, the Lord sent a revival of historic proportions to North America. It broke out at the Toronto Airport Vineyard Christian Fellowship, which is now called the Toronto Airport Christian Fellowship. People laughed, cried, fell, shook and saw their lives changed. A wide and deep river of the Father's love sprang forth and produced miracles of every kind. People came to Toronto and went home more in love with Jesus than ever before. Burned-out pastors and leaders from all over the world came to be filled with new hope and fresh fire. Planeloads of the spiritually hungry flew in from Great Britain, Europe, Asia, South Africa and a dizzying list of other points on the globe. Thousands took it home and lit the fire in other places so that unnumbered points of light sprang up all over the world.

A couple of years later, a pastor's wife from an Assembly of God congregation in Brownsville, Florida, went to Toronto, got blasted by the Spirit of God and took it home with her. Shortly thereafter, the great Brownsville revival took root and began to spread across the country and the world. Where Toronto had touched many who related to a Vineyard style of worship and ministry, Brownsville Assembly reached deep into traditional Pentecostal groups. Outbreaks of the Spirit followed in Smithton, Missouri, and a host of other sites. Eventually it came to my own Denver, Colorado.

My congregation immersed itself in the Toronto branch of that river early in February 1996 after my executive pastor and I visited Toronto in the fall of 1995. We brought it home with us and began to see among our own people what we had seen in Toronto as people laughed with joy, or wept, many falling and shaking under the power of the Lord. Lives were changed. As time passed we saw gold appear in teeth, heart-attack damage healed, a deaf ear completely opened and a lot more.

In June 1998, the Brownsville team came to Denver and lit a fire that burned for a while in a number of churches across the city, especially in traditional Pentecostal congregations. Wherever it went, traditional forms were trashed as God did wonderful things beyond the ability of human beings to control.

A Tragic Decision

Tragically, within a year of the visit of the Brownsville team to Denver, the fires began to burn measurably lower. I watched, grieving, as the Body of Christ in the city of Denver and across North America gradually made a collective decision with regard to the visitation God had sent. All across the continent, even as the outpourings in major centers like Toronto and Brownsville continued, cries for revival ascended to heaven but seemed to go unheeded. We longed to see our churches filled. We prayed to see salvations. We insisted that we hungered for the presence of God, but in truth we did not want all the "mess" that comes with the manifestation and presence of the Spirit of the sovereign God. Collectively the majority of the Body of Christ made a decision against revival.

What most of us meant in our cry for revival was, "Come, Lord, but keep it neat and clean." Never mind the disciples on the day of Pentecost, so weak in the knees and disoriented by the power and presence of the Spirit of God that the crowd which had gathered to gawk at them believed them to be intoxicated. Never mind Daniel on his hands and knees trembling physically as the angel of the Lord touched him. Forget the priests at the dedication of Solomon's temple who could not stand up to minister because of the glory present in the place. "Come, Lord, but keep it neat and clean. Do not do anything we cannot understand and control."

As the manifestations of revival died in Denver and the nation, that long period of natural physical drought of which I spoke in chapter 1 took hold in the Rocky Mountain region where I live and minister. It was historic in its proportions and especially prophetic in its implications.

During this time the Lord spoke to me about the wider Body of Christ in North America: *You cried out for revival. I sent you revival, but you did not like the way it looked!* With some stellar exceptions, North America as a whole refused what the few embraced. It was too messy. It was not what we wanted to see. It was too out of control. It did not serve "self." The Body of Christ cries for revival, but God already sent revival and His people did not like the way it looked. Sounds like a certain generation of Pharisees of Jesus' acquaintance, don't you think?

The drought continued, and I knew the river of the Spirit would not flow again until we humbled ourselves to receive it on God's own terms, and not ours.

His Plans, Not Ours

Over the years of walking with God, I have learned that He is not much interested in what I personally want, like or prefer. He is God. I am not. He is interested only in what is right and perfect, and He loves you and me enough to refuse to negotiate with us where the right and perfect are concerned. He stands firm on His own plans, focused only on what He wants, likes and prefers because He knows infinitely better than we do what we need. His plans work. Ours do not. His presence accompanies His own plan, not the plans and schemes of men and women. Although the wilderness can be a place of tremendous uncertainty, history teaches us that when His people follow the pillar of cloud by day and the pillar of fire by night, power manifests. The way through the wilderness is revealed.

Standing for Revival

Ever since immersing ourselves in the Toronto stream, my own church has fought a long and difficult battle to keep the well open and to remain in the Presence. We lost people at first. We have been maligned and accused by other Christians. The enemy has tried to destroy us. Ambitious and unbalanced disrupters came to exploit our freedom as a platform for their own agendas and then left us, hurling curses over their shoulders as they went. It was glorious and worth it but never easy. And we know of others who have fought the same battle.

The Father has used the years of struggle to deal with us, to cleanse us, to love us and to change us. When His Spirit floods in, evil flees out. It has been terribly, awfully wonderful. It has been delightful, and it has also been the suffering of the cross. We have hung on, determined to follow, determined to retain the wonders we had waited all our lives to see.

It was and is unpredictable and often messy, but we love it. We never know what God will do or how people will respond when He moves. We never know when He will "ruin" a meeting, or how we will have to adapt to accommodate Him. It is an adventure, and every one of us who has persevered in this river has been deeply changed for having embraced it and soaked in it. We have been moved by Him out of the culture of self to become a people engaged in outreach and giving for the sake of our community. The Holy Spirit comes not to join our culture but to change it!

"Up" the Expectations

Those who have stood for this revival and received it on God's terms need to ramp up their expectations of what the Lord is about to do. I always wonder if I am being presumptuous when I take a Scripture addressed to a particular church in a particular place in Bible times and apply it specifically to my own situation, but I believe the Lord told me this one belongs to us who have stood the ground. It applies to those who have fought for the outpouring of the Spirit as God gave it and did not back away:

> I know your deeds. Behold, I have put before you an open door which no one can shut, because you have a little power, and have kept My word, and have not denied My name. . . . Because you have kept the word of My perseverance, I also will keep you from the hour of testing, that hour which is about to come upon the whole world, to test those who dwell on the earth. I am coming quickly; hold fast what you have, so that no one will take your crown.
>
> Revelation 3:8, 10–11

An Hour of Testing and Release

An hour of testing is coming upon the Western church. In fact, it is already here. A great sorting out has begun and will intensify in the years to come. *Ichabod*—"the glory has departed" (see 1 Samuel 4:21)—will be written over the doors of many houses of worship where the culture of self has determined the agenda. God will dismiss leaders who serve the culture of self and fail to lead the people into the richness of His Spirit. He will give the sheep to those who will feed them on the true substance of both the Spirit and the Word, imparting to them the true meaning of the cross and the blood as these call us to sacrifice—the death of self as the means to life.

If the time to come is to be one of sifting and sorting, however, it also will be the finest hour of the Church for those who hear His Word, who know His Spirit and who have taken His selfless character into themselves. The Father has set before us an open door that no one can shut. The power and love we have known is about to become the power we give to others in ways we have not known and with levels of favor we could only imagine in times past.

For those who have stood the ground, an hour of release is coming—a time of sending that we might give away the wonder and the sense of His presence which the Lord has so carefully deposited over the years since 1994. We will see it realized as a harvest of souls in biblical proportions, as on the day of Pentecost. We will see it in miracles performed not only in church and conference settings, but also in the street and in the workplace where Jesus always intended our gifts to be employed. He Himself performed the overwhelming majority of His miracles of healing and multiplication in the public places, rather than behind the safe walls of the temple or the local synagogue. It was there that He met the needs of people and gave the love away. We will heal the sick, raise the dead and proclaim the Kingdom of God. In other words, we will do it where the world can see it and we will follow it up by explaining to the world what is happening and why.

We will have to cry out once again for a renewed visitation freed from the culturally based constraints and objections of the past. We will have to receive it as those who would give it away and not as consumers. It will require broken hearts, filled with repentance and saturated with the character of Jesus as we have absorbed it during these years of soaking in the current outpouring.

God sent His gift. Some of us received it, but collectively the Bride of Christ refused. Even among those who embraced what the Father sent, many lost it because they received it for the enrichment of self, as just another wonderful experience, rather than as the selfless power to witness that Jesus promised in Acts 1.

Collectively now, we in the Body of Christ who still hunger and thirst for more must possess a deep heart of repentance. We must plead in humility and brokenness of heart, "Mercy, Lord! Forgive us! We are sorry, Lord, for rejecting what You sent! We are sorry for that version of self-focus that caused us to cling to human control. Have mercy, Father, and let the lightning strike yet once more. Any way You want to come, we will humble ourselves to receive it. Any way you want to show Yourself, we will take it."

Then watch the power flow.

12

Reclaiming a Generational Destiny

———————————•———————————

Transcending the culture of self requires responding to a calling. It is the calling of a purpose greater than ourselves. Not one of us comes into the world without this calling. You were therefore born with a mission that calls you beyond yourself to a divinely ordained place in the Father's plan to expand the Kingdom of God and move the world toward eternity. The culture of self with all its distortions of life and ministry seeks to rob us of that calling; nevertheless, the calling is there, and it is not just for us, but for our children, their children and their children's children.

He Created You for Your Calling

"For we are His workmanship, created in Christ Jesus for good works, which God prepared beforehand so that we would walk in them" (Ephesians 2:10). For those works, you have been gifted and endowed with all the tools you need to get the job done, both from the Spirit of God and in your created nature. Romans 11:29 says, "The gifts and the calling of God are irrevocable," meaning that God does not change His mind concerning these gifts and callings. He will not fire you. He will not take back what He gave, withdraw the gift or invalidate the calling. It is the purpose for which you were created.

The dynamic of a life determined by a calling is that if you live in and for the calling, rather than for self, then emotional, relational and spiritual prosperity result. Godly purpose makes sense of life in a way that absorption in "things" or self never can.

It Requires a Demonstration of Commitment

"Do not store up for yourselves treasures on earth, where moth and rust destroy, and where thieves break in and steal. But store up for yourselves treasures in heaven, where neither moth nor rust destroys, and where thieves do not break in or steal; for where your treasure is, there your heart will be also."

Matthew 6:19–21

If your treasure—or investment—rests in a material vault rather than in your God-given calling, purposelessness results, because the heart rests in a place incapable of producing ultimate satisfaction. "I am a Christian and Jesus is the most important thing in my life" will not wash until you substantiate the claim by means of clear and visible demonstrations of commitment.

Callings Are Not Just for Individuals

If the truth of irrevocable calling applies to individuals, it also must apply to entire peoples and generations of people. Both nations and generations receive callings and gifts from God to carry out their callings. God will no more change His mind about these national and generational callings and gifts than He will change His mind about personal callings and gifts.

"The gifts and the calling of God are irrevocable" (Romans 11:29). This refers to the entire nation of Israel as a people and to their calling in and for the world. Individually we partake of it, but the calling itself is shared. When God calls and gifts a people, nation or generation, He cannot and will not change His mind or withdraw what He has given. We can forget about it, run away from it, reject it, lay it down and rebel against it, but the gifts and the calling remain.

Our Calling Is Generational

Israel's calling—and that of the Church in our generation—was and is multigenerational, designed to be passed on as an inheritance to our children:

"Now this is the commandment, the statutes and the judgments which the LORD your God has commanded me to teach you, that you might do them in the land where you are going over to possess it, so that you and your son and your grandson might fear the LORD your God, to keep all His statutes and His commandments which I command you, all the days of your life, and that your days may be prolonged. . . . You shall teach them diligently to your sons and shall talk of them when you sit in your house and when you walk by the way and when you lie down and when you rise up."

Deuteronomy 6:1–2, 7

God gives vision, calling and purpose with a three-generational component. We must teach it to our sons and daughters, but in a way that enables them to pass it to the third generation—"you and your children and your children's children" (Deuteronomy 6:2, NRSV). The purposes of God in our day cannot be accomplished by any one generation, but only by the generations together. Jeremiah 31:13 sings of the young and the old dancing together and connects it with joy and abundance for the people of God. According to Malachi 4:5–6, the curse of God is avoided by the coming together of fathers and their children. It is a shared destiny. I fear that too many of us have given birth to our children not to send them as arrows into the heart of our enemy, but for the sake of our own self-fulfillment. The culture of self would have taught us that.

God promised Abraham (in Genesis 12 and other places) that his descendants would become a great nation and that in him all the families of the earth would be blessed. From the beginning, the people of God were blessed to be a blessing beyond themselves. Through Abraham came the revelation of the one God. Through Abraham came Moses, who established the revelation of God's will as expressed in Scripture. Through Abraham came King David and ultimately Jesus. Through Jesus came salvation, the Holy Spirit and relationship with Father God, and through Jesus all the nations of the world obtain a blessing. In Abraham and his descendants, we see a destiny and a calling larger than themselves, passed from one generation to another and resulting in a great and glorious realization of the purposes of God. It began with a calling and a gifting for a whole people, and it remains the plan of God for His Church today.

Samson: A Generational Parable

In Judges 16, with no central government and no standing army, Israel suffered devastating attacks by the Philistines on a regular basis. In the face of this threat, God anointed judges to lead and protect the Israelites. Among them was Samson, born a Nazirite and dedicated to God from birth. From his uncut hair flowed gifts of incredible strength and skill in battle. His exploits became legend. With nothing but the jawbone from a dead donkey, he killed a thousand Philistines single-handedly. With his bare hands, he pulled the gates of cities out by the posts. No rope held strength enough to bind him. The Philistines were terrorized.

Though he bore a calling and a gift to serve the whole people of God, Samson allowed himself to be seduced by a loose Philistine woman named Delilah. Employing every time-tested feminine wile in the book of sex and seduction, Delilah coaxed from him the secret of his strength.

> She made him sleep on her knees, and called for a man and had him shave off the seven locks of his hair. Then she began to afflict him, and his strength left him. . . . Then the Philistines seized him and gouged out his eyes; and they brought him down to Gaza and bound him with bronze chains, and he was a grinder in the prison.
>
> Judges 16:19, 21

193

Hear well the lesson! Those who abandon the calling of God and lay down the gifting bestowed by Him become blind and weak. Imprisoned in a dark world of self-focus, they wander in circles like Samson at the grinding wheel, without direction, trapped in futility. No longer do they see or perceive the presence of God as they once did. Light and joy grow dim. Because the grinding wheel of life weighs heavy and the work lacks meaning, depression sets in. This was what happened to Samson, and this is what happens to every servant and generation of servants who abandon or trade the calling of God and His gifts for some other pursuit.

But God does not change his mind, no matter how far we fall. He will never cancel the contract or nullify the covenant. The calling waits, held in reserve against the day of our return. So Samson's hair grew until the day when the Philistines desired to make a public spectacle of him, this man who had once so bested them in battle. Three thousand men and women filled the temple of Dagon filled with anticipation of a day of fun at Samson's expense.

> Then Samson called to the LORD and said, "O Lord GOD, please remember me and please strengthen me just this time, O God, that I may at once be avenged of the Philistines for my two eyes." Samson grasped the two middle pillars on which the house rested, and braced himself against them, the one with his right hand and the other with his left. And Samson said, "Let me die with the Philistines!" And he bent with all his might so that the house fell on the lords and all the people who were in it. So the dead whom he killed at his death were more than those whom he killed in his life.
>
> Judges 16:28–30

In the end, Samson reclaimed what had been his all along. The gifts and the calling of God are irrevocable.

A Revolutionary Calling

I am 53 years old at this writing and part of an age group that I believe constitutes a "Samson generation" in this day. Samson's life stands as a parable of who and what we were to be, how we have fallen and what we must become again.

God sent us into this world with a calling beyond ourselves as a generation of revolutionaries destined to change things. Joel 2:28 and the verses that follow tell us that in the last days He will pour out His Spirit on all flesh, which means not just believers, but the unbelieving world as well. All means *all*. And with the outpouring of His Spirit come His gifts and purposes.

Understand that God showers gifts even upon those who do not know Him. These gifts may be misused and misunderstood, but they remain His gifts. Satan creates nothing; he is the destroyer, not the Creator, and can only twist what God gives and distort what God creates.

We as a generation, therefore, began to both use and misuse our generational gifting. On the good side, we did change the world. We marched for civil rights. We brought down the Jim Crow laws in the American South, ending our American version of apartheid. Gone are separate drinking fountains and restrooms for blacks and whites. Gone is the requirement that black Americans ride at the back of the bus and enter buildings by the back door. We integrated schools, colleges and workplaces and ensured equal access to the vote for all races. Without the revolutionary anointing of this generation, these things would never have been possible.

We revolutionized music forever, creating genres and styles that had never before existed. Rock. Folk rock. Folk styles that varied from the norm. Fresh harmonies, chord progressions and beats. Guitar evolved into an instrument never before conceived. Much to our elders' chagrin, we changed the way the whole culture looked and felt. It ranged from the sublime to the ridiculous, but we had a revolutionary impact on our world.

In the midst of it all, in response to the desperate prayers of a generation of concerned Christian parents, the Jesus Movement broke out—first in Southern California, then spreading quickly through America and the Western world. The "all flesh" anointing became a holy one for those who came to know Jesus, and as a result it began to accomplish the revolution for which it really had been given. As we reached beyond ourselves to share what we had been given, tens of thousands of young people came running to Jesus.

We were just kids with nothing more to work with than the figurative jawbone of an ass, as we drove around in our smoking Volkswagon microbuses covered with flowers and poems, wearing ragged jeans and singing Jesus songs with beat-up, out-of-tune guitars. But in spite of our youth and ignorance, people fell all over themselves to come to Jesus.

Even those who rejected the message respected our passion and zeal. In 1971, I attended a rock festival at Farragut State Park in northern Idaho, where twenty thousand largely naked and semi-naked young people danced to the music of one of the secular bands singing, "Well, hurray for the Jesus people! At least they know just where they're at!" It was a holy revolution in a revolutionary time! Even the unbelieving world stood up and took notice!

When they did not readily line up to get saved, we went out and compelled them to come. That same year, 1971, I was home from college in the summer and living in Wallace, Idaho, working deep in the hard rock mines to earn money for the next school year. Wallace was a pretty boring place, so on weekends I drove to Spokane, Washington, about an hour and a half away. The Jesus Movement had reached its vibrant peak there, and I could always find some believers to hang out with. We would form "posses" to invade the parks where the drug dealers were most active. Four or five of us would find some soul to pursue, back him or her into a corner and press in until the person gave his or her life to Jesus. And it did not stop there. The group made certain he or she got discipled in the days that followed.

We ganged up on our friends, refusing to allow them any peace until they came with us to hear the Gospel or attend a Christian concert. Our music was cutting edge, speaking directly into the culture to reap a harvest of souls. Why? Because the musicians were fresh out of the world, wildly in love with Jesus and not yet stifled by the religious spirit that would infect us later.

We revolutionized the Church. Until that point, all the churches sang old hymns accompanied by organs and pianos, completely missing the culture around them. Our generation changed all that, even in the face of being labeled "of the devil" for doing it. Today contemporary Christian music can be heard every Sunday in almost any church of any denomination or tradition.

I find it amusing that, like Samson, the calling card of our generation was long hair. I got kicked out of school more than once for refusing to cut mine.

How We Lost It

God intended that our generation remain in that revolutionary and world-changing calling—that we would lead our children into it and pass it on to them as a Deuteronomy 6 inheritance. It should have been a three-generational vision, a burning purpose beyond ourselves passed on to those who came after us, something we would pursue and share together.

Instead, like Samson, we allowed ourselves to be seduced by the culture around us, the culture of self that had grown up with us even as we fought to change our world, and we both literally and figuratively cut our hair. The lusts of the world drew us in by means of the Baal of self-fulfillment until we lost our vision in the dark mists of the pursuit of mammon.

Few of us could point to any moment in time when we lost it. We would never consciously have surrendered ourselves in that way. It happened slowly, by degrees, under the insidious and gradual pressures of the job, the house, the car and the money to pay for it all. Things so many of us once despised our parents for pursuing with such urgent dedication became necessities for us as well.

At least we thought they were necessities, and so we began to invent that complex latticework of teachings that told us how to work the principles of God in order to be healthy, wealthy and wise. In doing so we lost the vision of the cross and self-sacrifice and called it all "Christian." Baal seduced us and led us away in chains to the grinding wheel of lives lived for self. We laid down our calling and gifting and fell asleep on Delilah's knee.

There the curse came upon us just as it came upon Samson, and like him we became blind, lost, weak and imprisoned. No longer did we speak of conquering the world or changing it for Jesus. Our life focus had shifted elsewhere.

When the transcendent purpose that had once filled our lives failed, so did our marriages—at the same rate statistically as those in the world. We grew ever more depressed as a generation. Never in the history of the Western world have so many sought counseling and therapy. The most popular teachings in Christendom have not been how to win the lost, change the world and be given away in love. They have been about personal healing, inner healing, marriage classes and other remedial and self-oriented stuff.

Our churches stopped growing, and we began to leave them in droves—disillusioned, unhappy and wondering where we lost that wonderful sense of the Lord that had so driven us in our youth. When some of us at last came back to the Church, we returned often to choose churches with truncated worship and watered-down preaching that neither challenged us nor took us into the presence of God.

God sent the prophetic movement in the 1980s, intending for it to inject life into us and set us back upon the course of our destiny, but we twisted it to serve our now entrenched generational self-absorption. As I have already said, prophetic ministry should have equipped and motivated us for the mission, releasing power for change, as Ephesians 4:11 teaches. It should have plucked up and planted, torn down and built up, according to Jeremiah 1:10. We should have seen the structure of our cultural self-centeredness fall to rubble. We should have risen to revolutionary fervor for the Kingdom of God once again.

Instead we lined up to get personal words for our sad and futile lives—mostly what I have called "sanctified psychic reading"—rather than the life-changing and destiny-setting stuff of Scripture. We desperately longed to hear that a great purpose for our lives yet lay before us, that God had a calling and a direction for us. Why? Because we knew instinctively that we had lost it. The house, the car, the job and the marriage turned out to be insufficient to satisfy us—too small a purpose to sustain our lives—and so we listened eagerly to the words of all those emerging prophetic people. But we did it through the filter of self that we had so deeply learned for so long a time.

Our Children Paid the Price

What came next was tragic. Instead of handing our children a fiery passion, a revolutionary mission and purpose burning in their hearts as it had in the days of our own youth, we delivered them purposelessness and futility wrapped in gilded cages of nice homes, televisions and automobiles. Now they pay the price for our own aimlessness as we wander in circles, chained to the grinding wheel of self-focus in our spiritual and emotional blindness. Baal and Molech devoured Israel's children, too.

My son tells me that many of our youth cut themselves with knives, razors and glass because they have no other means of expressing their pain. Their parents do not know. They are too self-absorbed to know. Our children drink and do drugs under no delusions that it is going to expand their minds. Remember that one? How we deluded ourselves!

On August 29, 2004, we baptized twelve high school youth at our church. Only three parents bothered to come to witness this most important event in the lives of their children.

Some of the youth at our church do not smell so good. My son says it is because their parents allow them only one shower a week. They do not want to spend the money for all that hot water.

One young girl got pregnant the week before she graduated from high school. Her parents kicked her out of the house for her eighteen-year-old boyfriend to care for. He repeated his freshman year of high school three times and did not bother to show up for the fourth. No high school would allow him to enroll after that.

Four brothers live in an unheated and unfinished basement while their father keeps a nice spare room empty on the main floor of their home. The stories are endless and not at all uncommon.

I have spent hours helping my son work through his judgments on the incredible self-absorption of our generation. Every day my two daughters struggle with the destroyed lives of many of their young adult friends who share the same generation of parents who raised the teens we see in the youth group. Every day they grieve the damage done to the small children who are now the third generation.

I hear that 85 percent of youth raised in the Church will leave permanently upon graduation from high school. Personal observation confirms the truth of it. Our cultural self-absorption has given them no transcendent vision to make sense of their faith.

Taking It Back

But here is the good news: It is not over. God has not changed His mind about us. The gifts and the calling of God are irrevocable. As He did with Samson, God will return to us our strength and restore us to our calling, if only we will choose to respond to the call, renounce the culture of self and determine to move forward in sacrificial union with Jesus. Like the sudden bursting of a dam, we will see a release of power and calling upon our children and upon their children that will change their lives and ours more dramatically than we saw so long ago when we ourselves were still young. We will finally be "you, your son, and your grandson" going forth as a mighty army to win and change the world as we were always called to do, and as we once understood how to do before we lost our way and forgot. It is still there, all of it, hidden deep in our damaged souls, written indelibly into our spiritual and emotional DNA. All we have to do is remember to resign the service of the demon Baal, who masquerades as our beloved Lord, and respond.

When we respond, the generations will be healed in purpose, and together we will win more souls, drive out more demons, work more wonders and take more territory for the Kingdom of God than in all our lives before—just like Samson in the temple of Dagon. The early 1970s will pale in comparison.

The call has been issued. The Heart of Grace calls us in love. The Father of Light has issued the summons. Pick it up! Recover what was lost! Believe the promise that whoever loses his or her life for Jesus' sake will find it! God has not changed His mind about us! Let us give it back to our children and grandchildren. Let us once again change the world!

> "Then the virgin will rejoice in the dance,
> And the young men and the old, together,
> For I will turn their mourning into joy
> And will comfort them and give them joy for their
>   sorrow.
> I will fill the soul of the priests with abundance,
> And My people will be satisfied with My goodness."
>
> Jeremiah 31:13–14

The promise is three-tiered—the generations together. But the young do not want what we have now. Would you? They want what we once had, before the culture of self deceived us and robbed us of our sense of purpose.

We must pick up our calling once again, and in so doing, give the young something to unite behind. Only when the generations "dance" together in worship and ministry will the Church find its true glory. In my city the two most prominent African American pastors, Acen Phillips and Bishop Phillip Porter, have passed their churches to their sons and have gone on to greater ministries in the wider Body of Christ, while remaining a vital part of the ministries their sons now lead. When John Osteen died, whom many of us know from his televised sermons, his son Joel took over the ministry without so much as a wrinkle or a stutter. These stand as prototypes of what God Himself wishes to restore to His people. Only a purpose larger than self can serve to inspire our children and redeem an entire culture.

> "Behold, I am going to send you Elijah the prophet before the coming of the great and terrible day of the LORD. He will restore the hearts of the fathers to their children and the hearts of the children to their fathers, so that I will not come and smite the land with a curse."
>
> Malachi 4:5–6

We must stand together, young and old, united around the common destiny—the calling and gifting of God concerning which He has never changed His mind.

Together, let us be revolutionaries who will not be told no, who will not be imprisoned and who will not be held back—an army of the Spirit-filled, focused beyond ourselves for the sake of others. It is past time to change the world once more. Like Samson, we must at the last recover what we laid down at the first and once again give ourselves away in loving and fearless sacrifice. In the last days, let us do more damage to the kingdom of darkness than in all our lives before—a Samson generation, restored in purpose and given in love, victorious over the culture of self.

203

Loren Sandford, with an M.Div. from Fuller Theological Seminary, has served four churches full time. He successfully planted two of those churches, including New Song Fellowship in Denver, Colorado, where he currently serves as senior pastor. In 1979 and 1980, he directed Elijah House, an international ministry in Christian counseling and counselor training founded by his parents, John and Paula Sandford. He continues to be in demand internationally, primarily for teaching but also for leading worship.

64275566R00115

Made in the USA
Lexington, KY
02 June 2017